HOW TO HAVE MORE MONEY NOW

EVEN IF YOU'RE STRUGGLING TO PAY THE RENT

Copyright © 2022 by Ruth Barringham
Published in Australia

The author is the copyright owner of this work, and no part may be reproduced by any process, nor may any other exclusive right be exercised without the permission of the Author.

This book is sold subject to the condition that it shall not, by way of trade or otherwise, be lent, re-sold, hired out, published electronically online or otherwise circulated without the Author's prior consent. All instances of copyright infringement will be dealt with to the full extent of the law.

The Author is not a lawyer or an accountant and does not intend to render legal, accounting, or other professional advice within this book. No guarantees of income, sales or results are promised. It is recommended that users of this book seek legal, accounting, and other independent professional business advice before starting any business or acting upon any advice given herein.

ISBN: Paperback: 978-0-6454502-4-8
       Ebook   978-0-6454502-5-5

Book cover image courtesy of Oleksandr/stock.adobe.com

Also by Ruth Barringham

How to Quit Smoking
How To Write An Article In 15 Minutes Or Less
Goodbye Writer's Block
7 Day eBook Writing and Publishing System
Living The Laptop Lifestyle
Mission Critical for Life
Self Publish Worldwide
The 12 Month Writing Challenge

The Monthly Challenge Writing Series

Book 1 - Quick Cash Freelance Writing
Book 2 - Build A Lucrative Niche Website
Book 3 - Fast & Profitable Article Writing
Book 4 - The One Month Author

See more of my books on my website
https://ruthiswriting.com

Disclaimer:

The Author and Publisher have used their best efforts in preparing this book. The Author and Publisher make no representation or warranties with respect to the accuracy, applicability, fitness, or completeness of the contents of this book.

The Author is not a lawyer or an accountant and does not intend to render legal, accounting or other professional advice within this book. No guarantees of income, sales or results are promised. It is recommended that users of this book seek legal, accounting, and other independent professional business advice before starting any business or acting upon any advice given herein.

The information contained in this book is strictly for information purposes. Therefore, if you wish to apply ideas contained in this book, you are taking full responsibility for your actions. Whilst we hope you find the contents of this book interesting and informative, the contents are for general information purposes only and do not constitute advice. We believe the contents to be true and accurate as at the date of writing but can give no assurances or warranty regarding the accuracy, currency, or applicability of any of the contents in relation to specific situations and particular circumstances.

This book is not intended to be a source for advice, and thus the reader should not rely on any information provided in this book as such. Readers should always seek the advice of an appropriately qualified person in the reader's home jurisdiction. The Author and Publisher of this book assume no responsibility for information contained in this book and disclaim all liability in respect of such information. In addition, none of the content of this book will form any part of any contract or constitute an offer of any kind.

Any links to third party websites are provided solely for the purpose of your convenience. Links made to websites are made at your own risk and the Author and Publisher accept no liability for any linked sites. When you access a website, please understand that it is independent from the Author and

Publisher and the Author and Publisher have no control over the content of that website.

Further, a link contained in this book does not mean that the Author or Publisher endorses or accepts any responsibility for the content or the use of such website. The Author and Publisher do not give any representation regarding the quality, safety, suitability, or reliability of any of them or any of the material contained within them. Users must take their own precautions to ensure that what is selected for use is free of such items as viruses, worms, trojan horses and other items of a destructive nature.

All websites, products and services are mentioned, without warranty of any kind, either express or implied, including, but not limited to, the implied warranties of merchant ability and fitness for a particular purpose.

Table of Contents

Disclaimer: 7

Table of Contents 9

Introduction. 11

Chapter 1. How to Have More Money Now 19

Chapter 2. Garbage In. Garbage Out 22

Chapter 3. How to Make Budgeting Interesting? 25

Chapter 4. Dealing with Creditors 35

Chapter 5. Budgeting on Autopilot 38

Chapter 6. Food Budgeting 41

Chapter 7. Understanding Your Electric Bill 51

Chapter 8. Kids and Saving Money 61

Chapter 9. Cost Per Use 69

Chapter 10. Retail and Resale 75

Chapter 11. Free Days Out 78

Chapter 12. Gift Giving 81

Chapter 13. A Sufficient Abode 87

Chapter 14. To Work Full-Time or Part-Time 94

Chapter 15. Financial Round Up 99

Introduction.

Welcome to this guide on how to have more money, not just now, but for the rest of your life.

What we're going to be looking at are ways you can spend less, earn more, and if you're really struggling, how to get money right now. And not only will this give you a better life, but you'll have a ton of fun doing it too.

But, let me be clear. I'm not an accountant and I'm not offering any financial advice. I'm just going to share with you how I improved my whole life once I started looking at money in a different way, and how it's still helping me today.

And I turned my life around years ago when I was a single parent on welfare.

Everyone used to ask me how I managed to live so well with so little money. One guy said to me, "Me and my wife both work, yet you seem to live better than us on welfare. How do you do it?"

Well, the answer is a simple one.

It all began one day when I had a slap-your-forehead "Aha!" moment that changed my life. It made me realise that I wasn't as broke as I thought. I was just looking at it all wrong.

And now I'm going to tell you what it was that instantly helped me to have more money.

I call it:

The Ice Cream Story.

This is the story of how I landed myself alone and in debt with no idea whatsoever how to get out of it.

Not only that, but I knew that I was also about to lose my home as well.

I was a single mother of a 4-month-old baby left on my own, deeply in debt with the bank about to repossess my house.

How did I get into this situation?

I married the wrong guy. An alcoholic who drank away all our money.

That was in the 1980s.

Thankfully I've moved on since then by getting myself out of debt, finding myself somewhere else to live and never going back to that situation ever again.

But it was a slow process because not only did I physically need to change my situation, I also had to figure out how to do it.

One option was to go back to living with my parents. My mother was all for it but there was no way I was going to take a step backwards.

I was a single mother and I wanted to move forward with my life.

But first, I had to deal with finding somewhere to live and getting back in control of my finances.

It wasn't easy at first because I didn't know what to do. I didn't have a book like this to read to help me. I just had to figure it out.

I needed to know what to do to get out of the situation I was in as well as make sure it never happened again. Although, getting rid of the alcoholic husband was the first step.

When we first met I thought nothing of the fact that he always wanted to go out for a drink every night, especially given that his parents owned a pub.

But it never occurred to me that once we got married he'd still want to go out every night instead of staying at home.

We never kept alcohol in the house so my then husband would go out to work and instead of coming home, he'd go out for a drink...or two...or too many.

In those days wages were paid in cash so he always had money in his pocket. He never handed over all the money he earned, pretending that he'd borrowed from someone at work and had to pay it back or that he'd run up a bill in the works' canteen and had to repay it.

I was working too until we had a child and I still struggled to pay everything. I quickly went back out to work part-time after giving birth, but childcare costs literally ate away most of what I earned.

So, four months later, the mortgage was in arrears and our bills were too. The only reason our electricity wasn't cut off was that it was illegal for companies to do that if there was an infant living at the property.

But each month our bills and the mortgage got further and further behind.

Until one day I'd had enough and told him to leave. I could see no point in us carrying on.

He'd got us into so much financial difficulty that my feelings for him had waned to the point of indifference. I didn't care if he was there or not and considering how much he drank, I was better off without him, no matter how much dire straits that would leave me in.

So off he went, and I sat down with the biggest feeling of relief. I had no idea what I was going to do, but one thing was for sure.

I was completely in control of my life. I couldn't control things when there was someone else messing things up, but once he walked out the door, I regained control. I thought that even if the worst happened and I lost the house and had to go and live with my parents, it would only be temporary, and I'd still be in control of my life.

At first I tried to keep working part time but it wasn't enough money, so I had to apply for welfare.

And that made me cry.

Not because I had to live on welfare, but at how little they paid.

It wasn't enough to pay my mortgage and my bills, let alone being able to afford to eat and buy clothes.

At the time I was living in the UK. My parents had moved the family there from Australia a few years previously.

The Welfare payments I was to receive were only 32 British Pounds a week, which is about $64. I'll talk dollars from now on to make it easier to understand.

How on earth was I supposed to survive on $64 a week. I was also automatically entitled to monthly family benefit payments that anyone with children was allowed to receive but that was only about $25. Still not enough to live on.

I had to do something. And I had to do it quickly.

But what?

What was I supposed to do when I didn't have enough income to live on? And the mortgage payments were already in arrears and if I didn't do something about it, I'd lose my home.

Eventually everything worked out for the best. But it took some figuring out on my part.

But I found somewhere to live that was within my budget, moved, paid off all my debt, and began my life over with a plan in place to not only get out of debt, but to live well.

And I did it. It was actually quite simple.

It was a few years later, in the 1990s. I had a desk at the front window, and every afternoon I'd sit there, get out my money journal (which was a notebook that I'd drawn up into columns for income and outgoings) and write down everything I'd spent that day, down to the last cent.

I'd sit there and diligently go through my receipts and write it in my money journal.

Then I'd look at how much money I had left, which bills were due and when my next welfare payment was due, which came weekly.

I was smart enough to keep a track of my bills and make sure I kept enough back each week so that I'd be able to pay them. But it was still depressing trying to balance such a tiny budget.

I was, at that time, studying for a degree on the Open University, which was free to do, and I could study at home so I didn't have to pay for childcare.

The welfare system still didn't pay much, but if I went out and worked for minimum wage and paid childcare, I'd only be $5 a week better off. So I figured my best option was to study and get a high-paying career instead. But I was still a couple of years off from finishing my degree, and I needed money now.

Then the Aha! moment suddenly hit me.

Every afternoon a 'Mr. Whippy' ice cream truck would come down our street and stop in front of my house. This truck came 7 days a week, and every single day, the woman across the road (who was also a single parent on welfare) would come out with her two young sons and buy them each an ice cream.

Usually, I'd look up briefly and then go back to crunching my tiny numbers. But this particular day I watched her, and I thought, "How the hell does she afford two ice creams a day when I can barely afford groceries?"

I kept watching her this day. The ice cream truck drove away and she went back across the road to her house. On the inside front window there was one big curtain hanging sloppily on a piece of string, and I thought, "She could probably afford to buy a curtain rail if she stopped wasting money on ice creams."

And that was the Aha! moment. I realised that she could afford to buy a curtain rail, and a lot more, if she didn't buy two ice creams every day.

Right then and there, I got out a piece of scrap paper and started to do the math. Two ice creams a day, 7 days a week at $2.50 per ice cream, added up to $35 a week.

Holey Moley! That was a lot of money. Plus, I often saw her, at least once a week, walking back from town and her kids each had a packet of potato chips and a bar of chocolate or some sweets.

Again, I did the math. $10 a week on chips and chocolate, plus $35 a week for ice cream was $45 a week. And that was a conservative estimate.

Over a year (52 weeks) she was spending $520 on chips and chocolate and $1,820 on ice cream which was a staggering $2,340 spent on junk.

I sat back in my chair and stared at those figures. I knew she was wasting money on these things, but I had no idea just how much. I was flabbergasted at how easy it is to waste thousands of dollars every year and not even realise it.

But what about me? Was I wasting money too? I always considered myself to be quite a frugal person, but what if I was wasting thousands of dollars every year too?

That started me on a mission to take a good look at what I was spending my money on all the time.

I took out my receipts from the last month and looked at everything I'd bought. I wasn't just looking at how much I'd spent, but what I'd bought. To my horror I saw lots of processed junk food that was not only expensive but was bad for your health too.

I also realised my budget didn't include everything which was probably why some weeks were harder to balance than others.

I'd already proven from the cost of a daily ice cream how quickly things add up from seemingly insignificant amounts of money.

And being on welfare meant that I already had a tight budget, but I needed to tighten it even more.

From what I'd already learnt, $10 saved every week was an extra $520 a year, and at the time I was getting less than $100 a week so having an extra $520 was huge. And if I cut back and saved $20 a week, that would be an extra $1040 a year.

This was a life-changing moment for me.

I knew I'd have to reduce the grocery budget, but I'd also need to cut back spending in other ways too, including reducing the gas and electric bill.

That night my mind was buzzing with ideas at all the different things I could cut back on, so that we could live better. I stayed at my desk for hours crunching my numbers.

I turned out that it was not only easy to do, but it was fun too. It was so interesting to start living in a different, and better way, while I watched my savings add up.

I even found a way to have more money straight away. By the end of that first week I already had money in the bank, and a year later, I had thousands.

And I'll tell you how I did it.

Chapter 1.
How to Have More Money Now

On that first night of my mission to have more money and a better life, with my head buzzing with all the changes I was going to make, one of the things I was thinking about was what it was that I'd wasted money on over the years. Not just junk food, but things I bought that were wants, rather than needs.

I looked through all my cupboards and saw a huge number of things that I bought but hadn't used in years.

I also had appliances and furniture that were unused and unnecessary.

The next day I cleaned out all the cupboards. One by one I took everything out, cleaned the cupboard and only put back things that I really wanted or that were necessary. The rest I left in a pile in the living room.

I also went through my son's things and realised that he had far too many toys and a lot of them he never played with anymore because he'd outgrown them. So, they too were added to the pile. I also added the nest of tables and other pieces of furniture I never used, and most of my ornaments and other nick-knacks.

When I saw it all together, I was ashamed of how much money I'd wasted on these things. But they do say that we buy through our emotions, not our logic. That's why we see something in a shop and think we've just got to have it. It's purely an emotional response.

With my unwanted items gathered, I made a list of them and wrote next to each one what I thought I could sell it for. I knew that at the right price I could probably sell it all.

The only way to sell things back then was by putting a free ad in the local newspaper, or on supermarket notice boards, so that's what I did. And I sold everything in just a few days. It was a busy few days, but it was worth it, and I banked all the money I made, although it was so long ago I can't remember how much it was, but I do know it was several hundred dollars.

These days it's much easier to sell things on the internet or with a garage sale.

A few years ago, my (now) husband and I, (who I live with back in Australia) downsized from a house to a 2-bedroom apartment, so we had a lot of items to sell, including all our gardening equipment which we no longer needed.

I used Facebook marketplace to advertise it all. We also had a granny flat at our house so all the furniture in that had to be sold too.

It was amazing how quickly I sold it all and made over $2,000 too. One of my new neigbours at the apartment complex told me that she had sold everything she owned when she moved and used the money to buy new furniture for her apartment. She said she'd made over $6,000 from the sale of everything in her house. She said that whatever she had to sell, there was someone who wanted to buy it.

And that's what you do if you need money now. Go through everything in your home, including cupboards, wardrobes, garages and sheds.

Whatever you find that you don't want any more or you don't need, sell it.

When I was selling our stuff online, some items were sold and picked up withing an hour of me listing them.

If you're not sure how much to sell things for, look at similar items that others are selling to get an idea of price.

You can also have a garage sale if you have a lot to sell or if you have a lot of small items like books and garden tools and plant pots.

If you have any old or inherited items that you don't want it may be worth getting an antique dealer to value them. You might find that it's worth a lot more than you think.

You may also have a local pawn shop that will happily pay you for some of your items instantly.

Once you start looking at all the excess stuff you own and all the ways you can sell it, you'll find it easy to raise instant cash.

And making money from things you don't need is just the first step to having more money and a better life.

And next we'll look at a simple mind-shift that can save you thousands of dollars a year.

Chapter 2.
Garbage In. Garbage Out

There's a saying about computer programs and mathematical equations. GIGA. This stands for Garbage In – Garbage Out, meaning that the quality of what you get out, depends on the quality what you put in. So, a faulty computer program or an incorrect equation will provide bad results.

Garbage In Garbage Out can also be used for other things in life and can mean that better effort in anything you do brings better results.

When it comes to having more money, it can mean tracking your actual garbage.

This is how I look at it. We had two garbage bins outside when we lived in a house. One was for regular garbage, and the other was for recyclable garbage.

The regular bin had to be wheeled out to the curb for emptying every week. The recycle bin was emptied every fortnight. So, one week one bin was wheeled out and the next week both were wheeled out.

These were big bins that came up to my chest and I was appalled at how quickly people didn't just fill them, but overfilled them. So, I monitored our garbage for a few weeks and quickly saw the correlation between what we bought and how much garbage we had.

I also began to realise that anything that was over-packaged was cheap, and I don't mean in price, but the quality of the goods.

Over-packaging is the manufacturers way of making their products appear to be better than they are. And the excessive packaging quickly filled up our bins.

I decided to never buy heavily packaged products anymore. Even some food products are over-packaged. Easter eggs are a good example. The chocolate egg is wrapped in foil, which is placed inside a plastic egg-shaped packet which is then placed in a cardboard box.

The box often has cellophane windows too.

I figured out one day, that when you consider how thin and hollow these eggs are and how expensive they are, you're paying around $69 a kilo for chocolate. No wonder chocolate companies love Easter so much. Their chocolate eggs are more expensive than any other food in the supermarket.

Children's toys are often over-packaged too. I've seen small toy cars and dolls in packaging that's more than 3-times the size of the toy itself.

Household items can have too much packaging too, sometimes to make them look bigger or more expensive.

A few weeks ago, I bought a jaffle maker. The appliance itself is exactly 2 slices of bread wide and 1 slice of bread long, so it's quite small. But the box it came in was so wide I was struggling to carry it under my arm. I was walking home with it and had to keep switching arms. I was just glad that it was only cardboard that was holding it in place inside the box and not polystyrene. At least cardboard is recyclable.

So how I monitor my GIGO is that the less garbage in the bins the less I'm spending and the better-quality products I'm buying.

I buy unpackaged food from a zero-waste organic store. I take my own jars and paper bags and fill them up, so unless a bag rips, there's nothing to throw away and I know that we're eating good food.

And if we buy good quality household products and clothes (if we buy any at all), not only do they last longer than cheaper items, but there's less garbage in the bins.

We ended up with so little to throw away that we only put the garbage bins out once a month and most of the time they weren't full, but they were starting to smell because it's hot where we live, so we had to put them out to be emptied at least once a month.

We achieved this reduction in our Garbage Out by monitoring our Garbage In. Once we stopped bringing garbage into our home, we saved money in several ways: by not impulse buying cheap products, consuming less processed food, and our better-quality products last longer, so we don't have to buy them as often.

It's a win for our finances, our health, and the planet.

And all we did was reduce the amount of garbage we were producing.

Chapter 3.
How to Make Budgeting Interesting?

It's easy to think that budgeting your money is boring. But it doesn't have to be. If you do it right it can be really interesting.

It's all too easy to spend money, so easy that it's boring.

And what's the point of continually spending money on crap you don't need only to find out that by the end of the month, you've run out of money? That's an awful way to live, not to mention stupid. It's far better to do the mature and adult thing and don't overspend.

It used to be easier to budget when we only spent cash because you could see how much money you had. But with the "tap-and-go" way we live now it can seem impossible to track how much you're spending. But all you need to do is devise a financial budget so that you know your spending limits, and then be grown up enough to stick to them.

Where to Start

To begin, you need to list all the things that you spend money on now.

Start with the big things like your bills, including mortgage or rent, insurance, gas, electric, water rates, and council rates (local taxes). Write down how much they were over the last 12 months and how often you had to pay them (weekly, monthly, quarterly etc.)

Looking at your bills may sound dull, but it's quite interesting to see how much they cost over a year. In this group, also include debts that you're paying off, like car loan, credit card payments, etc.

Next comes your day-to-day spending which includes groceries, takeaways, car fuel, morning coffee on the way to work, clothes, alcohol, and everything else that you spend money on every week or month.

Group these things into Groceries and Extras

Now you should have 3 lists – Bills, Groceries and Extras.

Let's start with your bills.

These can be split into 2 lists – Ongoing and Temporary. The ongoing bills are the things that you need to pay no matter what, like electricity and rent. Temporary bills are things like loans and credit card debt, that will end one day.

Here is advice that you MUST follow.

DON'T GET INTO DEBT.

The only debt you should ever have, is a mortgage. Nothing else. Never, ever have any debt except a mortgage.

There are many ways to get into debt and too many opportunities with retailers advertising that you can have everything you want right now, even if you don't have the money to pay for it. Don't do it. Don't fall for these cons. If you can't afford it, don't buy it.

Before you even think about upgrading something you already own, ask yourself if it's necessary. Do you really need that new top-of-the-range $5,000, 65", TV on credit, or can you make do with your existing TV for another 12 months by which time the same new TV will have dropped in price (probably by 50%), or buy last year's model for $1,000? Or how about you just continue watching the perfectly working TV you already have?

Buying things on credit may feel like it's raising your lifestyle today, but it will lower it in the future.

It used to be that people only got into debt buying things they didn't need, but now even my local grocery store is offering a credit account to customers as an "easy" way to buy groceries. Yikes!

If you can't afford the groceries you want, buy cheaper ones. I remember years ago reading online about a guy who said, "I've always thought groceries were expensive till I realised pasta is only 99c a bag." Now that's using common sense. It's better to buy cheaper or less food than to go into debt to eat. And we'll look at exactly how you can drastically slash your food bill in Chapter 6.

For now, we're looking at your spending overall.

Your bills and debts are what you must pay, and you're stuck with them. But you can make it easier to pay them if you have the money ready.

Add up all your bills for the year. It will be frightening to see how much they're going to cost you for the next 12 months, but maybe that's a good thing, because it will show you how expensive debt is.

When you have your yearly amount, divide it by 12 (if you're paid monthly) to see how much you need to keep each month to cover them all. If you're paid fortnightly, divide it by 24 or for weekly by 52.

Make sure you've included everything in your ongoing bills list, like loans and credit card debt. If it's something you must pay for all the time, it must be included.

Reducing Multiple Debts

If you have multiple debts like more than one maxed out credit card or too many credit accounts and it's too much to pay them all, try reducing them using the snowball effect.

This works by listing your debts in order of how much you owe, from the smallest to the largest. Work on paying off the smallest one first. Do this by reducing your payments on the other debts to the minimum you have to pay. So, if you have a credit card debt, pay only the minimum balance, and use the extra money to pay off your smallest debt. Do this with each of your larger debts. Pay only the minimum and put the extra money towards paying off your smallest debt.

When the smallest one is paid off, repeat the process with your next smallest. Paying off debt is disheartening, but at least this way you can see the number of debts reducing and as you pay each one off, you can use the extra money to pay the next one off faster.

Regular Spending

Next you need to look at your regular spending which includes groceries, fuel, and anything else you buy regularly.

Anything that you buy from the supermarket, including groceries, cleaning items, washing powder, shampoo, toilet paper etc., comes under the grocery list.

Everything else comes under extras

You need to look at how much you spend on each of these monthly. Items in the extras list will change from month to month (or week to week, depending on when you get paid) but try to average it.

So now you know how much you spend per month on bills, groceries, and extras, so when you add them up you know how much it's costing you to live month to month. If it looks like more than you're earning, don't worry about it too much at this stage, because in the next few chapters we're going to go through each one and I'll show you an easy way to stay in budget so that not only will you have enough money to live on, but you'll be able to save money too.

For now, you need to look at other things that aren't part of your bills, groceries, or regular extras, and that is things like clothes, appliances, and cars.

These are things that you don't buy weekly or monthly, but you still need to buy them.

Clothes

These are easy. You already have a good idea of the types of clothes and shoes you need and how often you buy them.

Because you're looking at having more money, you must reduce your wardrobe down to only essentials. So, for the time being forget about expensive clothes or buying more of what you've got but never wear. Instead take a good long look at all the things you already own and figure out how you can go without buying anything else for at least a year.

If you have a wardrobe stuffed full of clothes and shoes that you've hardly ever worn, then you probably don't need to buy anything for a while anyway.

The best way to see everything you have is to take it all out, spread it out on your bed, then put it all back in piece by piece and arrange it all by type, so shorts together, shirts together, etc. You'll probably see that you've got more clothes than you thought, so your clothing budget for the next 12 months should be zero.

Appliances

These things aren't cheap and will need replacing at some point. You can include TVs, computers, and phones in this category too.

You need to make a list of all the necessary appliances that you own, and by necessary, I mean the ones you constantly use.

Next to each one write down what it would cost to replace it, you'll probably have to do an online search for this, especially if it's something you've had for years like a fridge or washing machine.

Make sure you don't leave any appliances off your list. If you own your own home include the built-ins such as oven and stove top.

Next to each price write how many years you expect each one to last. For instance, I wrote 6 years for my washing machine because that's the average of how each of mine have lasted.

My Vitamix (which I use a lot) came with a 7-year guarantee, so I wrote 7 years for that one.

Now that you know the price and expected life of each one, divide the price by the year of expectancy and then divide that by 12 to give you how much you need to put away each month to buy a replacement. Then, of course, add up all these amounts to get a total of what you need to save each month. You should find that it's not as much as you think and is probably only a few dollars a month.

Car

You may have a car now, but it won't last forever, plus there's the cost of upkeep. Hopefully you're smart enough to get it serviced every year to keep it running smoothly and to help stop unexpected huge repair bills.

I know that some people think that regular servicing is a waste of time and money, but I disagree. I've always had my cars serviced and not one of them has ever let me down. I had a small car that I gifted to a family member when I no longer needed it. The car was 6 years old and had been serviced every year. That car is now 12 years old and still running like a dream.

But cars don't last forever, or circumstances change, and we need something different. Either way it's best to be prepared because preparation is what having more money is all about.

So with your car, write down how much a yearly service costs, how much four new tyres cost, and what you pay for registration and insurance. Add those together and divide it by 12 for a monthly cost.

Once you know what that amount is, estimate how long you think your current car will last given its age and usage. Then divide the replacement cost by the expected future use of your current car for a yearly figure and divide it again by 12 for a monthly figure. This is how much you need to save every month to buy a new car for cash and not need to go into debt.

Add this to the previous monthly amount for running costs and that is what it will cost to keep you on the road.

If you have more than one car, then, naturally, you'll have to do the same again for your other car too.

Running two cars is a huge expense, and mostly unnecessary. If you do find that you live in such a way that you and your spouse both need to drive to get to work, then maybe it's time to rethink and move so that one of you is closer to work and doesn't need to drive or move closer to a train or bus station so that you're nearer to public transport. I once had a neighbour who told me that she'd never live anywhere that wasn't close to the shops, and near public transport. Not long after she told me that, her car was stolen. She collected the insurance money, but didn't buy another car, electing to get the bus to work instead and walk to the supermarket. Perhaps this could work for you too.

So now you have the amounts you need to save and buy new appliances and keep and afford a car.

Hopefully you're in position to not need new clothes for at least the next year. A zero budget is always the best, but when you do need to start buying clothes again, keep a clothing budget and save money every month so that when you do need to buy something the money is already there.

Groceries

When it comes to a grocery budget, it's different for everyone because it depends on the size of your family and their ages.

But regardless of that, you should try and have a zero-dollar budget. It's not easy because we all must eat, but if you start with a zero budget, then everything you buy is over budget, so it makes you more careful. If zero is too low for you, choose an amount that is as low as you can make it. Work out how much you spend per family meal, multiply that by 90 which is how many meals we eat in a month (3 meals a day x 30 days), add other items you buy regularly like toilet paper, shampoo, laundry soap, cleaning products, etc, to get an idea of how much you need to budget.

My grocery budget doesn't include meat or processed foods. Our meals are whatever we make from basic ingredients.

If we have a pie, it's a pie we made, not one we bought. The same goes for pizza. We also save money by making things that last more than one meal, like vegetable lasagna, stir fry, soup, or a casserole. These things are so cheap and can cost $1 per serving.

The reason we don't eat meat is because it's such a negative item. It's bad for our health (growth hormones, anti-biotics, stress of the animals, fat content, and more), so expensive to buy, bad for the environment (factory farming causes more pollution than all the cars on the roads) and so cruel to the animals.

Not only that, but it's an unnecessary food. No one has ever died from not eating dead animals.

The agricultural industry will try and tell you that eating animals is essential to good health, but that's not true. In fact, the opposite is true. People have overcome illnesses (including cancer) and obesity by giving up eating meat.

But you shouldn't take my word for it. Do your own research.

For now, look at your overall spending on groceries and see where you're going wrong.

What items have you bought recently that you didn't need to?

Whatever you normally spend at the supermarket, is there a way you can spend less? Are there items you don't need to buy?

Look at all the food in your pantry, fridge, and freezer. As you look at it all, make a note of all the meals you could make using nothing but what you already have. You'll be impressed with the results.

I did this recently and found that I already had enough items to make over 20 meals, and I consider myself frugal, so I bet you have a lot more already in your kitchen.

As an example, I found some dairy-free sour cream that needed using up, some potatoes in the fridge chiller drawer, and a bag of frozen winter vegetables in the freezer. So, the next night I baked the potatoes, split them open and topped them with boiled winter vegetables and sour cream. They were filling, cheap and delicious.

The following night I made a rice dish and cooked the rice in the vegetable water that I'd saved from the previous night's boiled vegetables for extra goodness and flavour.

If you have a good look through your own kitchen and make a note of all the breakfasts, lunches, and dinners you can make from what you already have, you may find that you don't need to shop for the next week or two, or that you need to buy very little.

This way, you can instantly reduce your food budget from several hundred dollars for the next week/month, to less than a hundred dollars, which is not only a huge saving, but it's extra money in your bank account instantly.

And in Chapter 6 we're going to look at how you can drastically reduce your grocery budget for good.

For now, there's just one more thing I want to touch on about budgeting, and that is personal money.

When we're kids, we're given pocket money which is money that we're allowed to spend on anything we want.

And that doesn't change when we're adults. We still want to have some money that's ours to spend on whatever we want, frivolous things that are not groceries or clothes or any other necessary items.

Therefore, you should still allocate yourself some personal money every month, which will be a lot more than when you were a kid. Having some personal money is even more necessary if you're a couple.

When I was single, I didn't worry about personal money because it was all my money. But when I got married, we pooled our money into a joint account and set up other accounts for our savings and bills, so it wasn't just my money to spend anymore.

That's why my husband and I each draw out our personal money each month and do with it whatever we want, although we probably spend half of it on eating out or going out for a drink. We don't do these things often, but it's surprising how quickly it adds up. Just one meal for two, with a couple of drinks can end up costing nearly $100, which is why we don't do it too often.

Chapter 4.
Dealing with Creditors

If you feel like you're drowning in debt because you have too many loans, too many credit cards, or you've opened too many credit accounts, it's an easy fix, but it does take time to sort out. But you got yourself into it, so now you have to get yourself out of it.

Imagine for a moment that you have no debt. You get paid every week/month, you put aside money for your bills and other expenses, buy your groceries, and you still have plenty left over for savings. Think about how great it feels to be so financially unburdened.

In fact, imagine how it would feel to have amassed so much money in savings, that if you lost your job, you'd have enough money saved to live on for a year or more. Can you imagine what that type of financial freedom feels like?

Well, that is what you're aiming for and it's why you need to make sure you deal correctly with your creditors, with the people/companies you owe money to.

In an ideal world, if you owe money, you have enough income to cover the repayments. But what if you don't? What if you've over-spent so much on your credit card and opened way too many credit accounts with companies that allow you to buy things now and pay for them later, and all the repayments are more than you're earning?

I found myself in this situation years ago when I split up with my alcoholic ex-husband who drank all our money away as well as taken out credit that we couldn't afford to pay back.

He did eventually leave, but the debt remained. We were even way behind with our gas and electric accounts.

So, I had to figure out what to do.

I was terrified of being taken to court and incurring court costs on top of everything else. But then I remembered that someone had once told me that they can only sue you if you don't pay them. They said no one can sue you for not paying enough, only for non-payment.

I had no idea whether that was true or not, but it sounded plausible, and at that time I could not afford to question it.

I sat down and worked out a weekly budget for myself. Then I looked at how much was left each week, which wasn't much, but I worked out how much I needed to pay each company to reduce the debt.

I then wrote a letter to each one, explaining my situation, that I was now a single parent with little money, but I was going to pay them every week till the debt was paid, and that I was going to set up automatic payments.

I then mailed the letters and set up the payments. I had no idea how each of them would react, and they all reacted the same, or more correctly they didn't react at all. I never heard anything from any of them. The payments kept going out automatically every week until the debts were all caught up, which took a couple of years, but then I was done, and my credit rating stayed intact.

I'm no financial expert, but I imagined that the reason my plan worked is because I dealt with my creditors the best way I could at the time and I guess it would have been hard for them, or probably impossible, to take me to court for paying as much as I could at the time. I let them know my situation immediately and kept up the small, but incredibly regular payments.

It wasn't easy at the time because it left me with such a small amount of money to live on.

In winter I'd go to bed early every night so that I didn't use electricity and heating. I tried everything I could to keep my bills low including making a sandwich for my lunch every day because it was cheap, and I didn't have to cook.

I went out for a lot of walks and spent hours in the local library to keep warm and not run up heating bills at home.

I was also fortunate at the time to have a few friends who also had babies, so I'd call in to see them and stay for coffee while my child played with theirs, and it was free to do.

And it all worked. My bills stayed low, my grocery bill was minute, and my debts all got paid.

The relief I felt when I finally paid them all off was immense. I could have paid less and paid them for longer, but I didn't want to do that. I felt that the financial sacrifice I made was worth it, even though I sometimes sat and cried at how hard it was to be so broke and be left with debts that weren't my fault.

If you're in the same situation, with an overwhelming amount of debts, my advice would be to try something similar to what I did.

Get a plan of how you can pay them off and get in touch with the companies and explain your situation and what you're doing to pay back the money.

Most importantly, make regular payments and don't miss any.

This may or may not work, but even if you do end up with a court summons, at least you can demonstrate that you're trying to put things right.

But in my experience (and that of others that I've known) all these companies want is their money. They don't want to go to court if they don't have to.

I found that if I was paying them regularly, even though it wasn't the full amount, they all were happy to leave me alone and let me go on paying.

Chapter 5.
Budgeting on Autopilot

In the last chapter we looked at getting in touch with creditors and companies you owe money to and making regular payments to them, even if it's lower than the amount you should be paying, to show good faith and reduce your debt at the same time. My only caveat with doing this is to ONLY do it if you are in financial distress. Don't get into debt just because you'd rather be spending your money on other things.

And now we're going to look at your ongoing debts which are those things you must pay regularly, like electricity, council rates/property tax, Netflix subscriptions and others.

You've already added up all these ongoing bills, so you know how much you need to save each week/month to pay them.

The way to make it simple is to put the money into a savings account that you use only for paying your bills, that way, whenever one comes in, you've got the money to cover it.

Some companies may offer the option of ongoing payments where they withdraw money from your bank account every month, so that when your bill arrives every quarter/half year, it's a statement instead of a demand for money.

I used to pay my gas and electricity bills this way and it was so easy. Plus, every 12 months they'd re-evaluate how much I was paying and how much gas and electric I was using, and because I was always trying to minimize my usage, my payments would often go down.

Paying with auto-payments was so incredibly easy. All I had to do was deposit the money into the account each week and the power companies took care of the rest.

Not all companies offer auto-payments like that, but if they do, it's something you should take advantage of.

The way I pay my bills now is similar. I still put the money into a savings account every month, only now it stays there until the bills arrive and then the companies also send me a date when they will be withdrawing the money from my savings account to pay for it.

It's still automatic payments, and all I had to do was sign a Direct Deposit form to allow the companies to take the payments from my account automatically when they're due.

It's easy to deposit the money into the savings account too because I do it online, and this too is automated.

Every week we go over our finance journal which is where we write down everything we spend. When we go shopping, or put fuel in the car, or buy anything, we enter it into the journal when we get home and leave the receipts with it. This way we know EXACTLY how much we're spending so that we never go over budget. It's also eye-opening to see how quickly small amounts of spending add up to large amounts. But this helps us to spend less because we're so aware of how easy it is to overspend, that we usually don't buy anything unless it's something necessary, and when you're always conscious about what you're spending, you quickly realise that most things in the stores are things you don't need.

Another way that setting up auto-payments helps is because the money for the bills goes straight into the savings account and so I never think about it. Every month it goes in automatically, and other money is automatically put into another account just for saving so is never touched.

The only money I deal with on a daily basis is the money in the general account which is only for groceries plus anything else we need to buy throughout the month like fuel for the car, wine, bits and pieces for the house, and anything else that comes up.

With our strict budget, we know exactly how much money is available to spend and we stick to it.

Chapter 6.
Food Budgeting

Let me make one thing clear. When I talk about buying food or groceries, that also includes other non-food items that we usually buy from the supermarket, like, baking foil, dish washing liquid, washing powder, toothpaste, toilet paper, in fact everything for the kitchen, bathroom and laundry that we use daily. You get the idea.

Food budgeting is a big part of living within your means. It's the biggest monthly expense after paying the mortgage/rent. But unlike the mortgage or rent, the amount you pay for food is up to you.

Paying for where you live is a fixed amount every month, so it's out of your control. What is in your control is where you live, so you can choose to live in a cheaper suburb and/or a smaller property.

Your regular grocery bill, while it too can vary on where you live, it's also controllable by where you shop and what you buy, so someone who buys a lot of steak and processed food, is going to pay two or three times more at the checkout than someone who buys a lot of rice, beans, and vegetables.

When it comes to food, don't fall into the trap of thinking that the more you spend the better you're eating. That could not be further from the truth. It's usually those who spend less and get more for their money that eat better.

Look at it like this, it's cheap, filling, and delicious to make a casserole, curry, or pasta dish in a slow cooker, and you can eat it with baked potatoes, rice, or garlic bread. And a one-pot meal like that will also provide enough left over for another meal. Win. Win.

Cooking from scratch is always cheaper and healthier than buying processed food.

I'm fortunate to be vegan, so I don't buy meat, which is not only bad for my health, but it's extremely expensive.

I've been vegetarian for a large part of my life and vegan for most of it. My husband was neither when I met him, but once he found out how delicious and varied a meat-free diet is, he was hooked. He said he previously believed, like most people do, that having a meat-free diet means that something is missing from it. I've always found the opposite to be true.

Our meals are incredibly varied, and we still eat things like pies and sausage rolls sometimes, but no animals are harmed in the making of them, and they are delicious with no chewy gristle or other unknown and unexpected things in the ingredients.

We also eat curries, chilli, spaghetti bolognaise, lasagna, pizza, soups, cakes and so much more. And the best thing is that it's all vegan and delicious. Whenever we have friends or family over for meals, no one notices that the food is vegan unless we mention it and then they're amazed.

What I'm trying to say here, is that you can significantly reduce your grocery costs if you cut out expensive items like meat.

The Australian Cancer Council states that eating red meat causes cancer and recommends avoiding eating barbequed meat and processed meats such as bacon and salami, as these are carcinogenic.

Not only that, but millions of people all over the world have cured themselves of cancer and symptoms of MS by changing their diet to organic vegan foods.

American Surgeon, Dr Neal Bernard has written many books on this subject and even helps cure his own cancer patients by getting them to change their diet.

There is a book I've read many times, Recalled by Life. By Dr Anthony Satillaro. He was dying of cancer and had only a few months to live and by chance he met a Macrobiotic Chef who told the doctor that he could cure his cancer if he followed a macrobiotic diet.

Because he had nothing to lose and was at the lowest ebb of his life, he followed the advice. At first, he became extremely ill as his body began to detox, but after a few weeks he felt better than he had in a long time, and his cancer went into remission until he was eventually cancer free.

A macrobiotic diet is extremely restrictive and is mostly brown rice, vegetables, and seaweed, but for advanced cancer sufferers it can be lifesaving.

Singer John Denver used to take a macrobiotic chef with him whenever he toured because he said it not only helped him keep his energy levels high, it also made him feel well and clear headed.

But don't just take my word about it all. There's plenty of information online and in books where you can discover more about it for yourself. On the last page of this book I've listed books by both doctors mentioned, plus other books mentioned throughout this one.

Besides all the health benefits to eating less (or no) meat, it can also save you a ton of money and can even halve the amount you normally spend.

The $21 Weekly Food Challenge.

There is a book called, 'The $21 Challenge,' that is all about how a family of four can survive on $21 a week for groceries. It's not advised to try this every week, but for one week (or even one month if you're really broke) and they say it will save you $300 a week (or $1,200 a month). If you want to see this book now there's a link to it, and to other books, on the last page.

The idea of the $21 Challenge is to eat for a week from the food you already have and use the $21 only for items you're desperate for, like milk or bread.

I've done this challenge more than once, so I know first-hand that it can be done.

The first thing you need to do is take a good look through all the places you keep food which are your pantry, fridge, freezer, and garden, and list the main items you find.

This stock take is amazing because it makes you realise how much food you already have without even realising it.

Next you go through your list and see what things go together for a meal, taking into account things for breakfast, lunch, and dinner.

I enjoy this part because it's like doing a puzzle, pairing things that can go together.

As an example, I recently did a stock take and found that we had a couple of kilos of potatoes that needed using up, So I cut them up, boiled them and we had boiled potatoes with our dinner that night, with plenty left over.

I put another meals-worth of boiled potatoes in a box in the fridge and mashed the rest.

The next night we had roast potatoes with dinner that I made from the box of saved potatoes, and the next morning we had potato cakes with breakfast that I made from the mashed potatoes (mixed with flour, patted into cakes, and fried), and I used the rest of the mash for topping homemade cottage pies.

I also found a can of condensed tomato soup, a packet of instant noodles, and two small bread rolls. I put the soup in a pan, added water, cooked the noodles in it, and we ate this noodle soup with a small bread roll each.

The way to reduce your grocery bill is to never let anything go to waste. If it's getting too close to its use-it-or-lose-it date, use it. Even if your vegetables are a bit limp, they can still be used in a stir fry or added to a casserole, or simply roasted.

My kitchen motto is "waste nothing." What's the point of buying new food if you've already got some that needs using up?

Here's my tip for not wasting food: Clean your fridge out every week.

Make it part of your weekly routine to take everything out of your fridge, clean all the shelves (just a quick wipe down will suffice if you do it regularly), and put everything back, checking dates on packaging, sniffing leftover food to determine freshness, and squeezing fruit and veg to see if it's still fresh.

Make a mental, or actual, note about what needs using up quickly, and do it.

Cleaning out the fridge once a week not only keeps it clean and smelling nice, but also saves you money by helping you use up items that you'd normally forget about until it's too late and you have to throw out.

Batch Cooking

This is an excellent way to save money on food and anyone can do it, even those who work full-time.

Decide what you're going to eat all week and prepare/cook it all in one go. If you work full-time, prepare your lunches for the week on Sunday and put it in boxes in the fridge so all you have to do is grab a box each day and take it with you. I know some people who prepare a whole month's worth of lunches and keep them in the freezer. But I've never gone that far.

Batch cooking not only makes it easier by doing all the cooking at once, but it also saves money because you're heating up the oven once to cook several things at once, and cooking a large pan of food once instead of heating up one small pan several times.

I personally love eating up food from the fridge, especially when it's putting together a meal from leftovers from other meals, because it's easy to reheat things. I don't have to prep things from scratch, and I don't have to think of what to cook, I just choose from what's already available.

Spend Less at The Checkout

Reducing your grocery budget is one of the things that you do have a lot of control of, plus as I previously said, it's the biggest expense after paying the mortgage/rent.

Sometimes it surprises me that some people don't even have a budget for food, which is probably why they constantly overspend.

Whatever your grocery budget is now, see if you can reduce it by at least 30%. Eventually it will be easy to cut it by 50% overall.

When you go shopping take a list with you of all the things you need.

We have a small white board on the door of our fridge/freezer and whenever we use the last of something, or it's running low (coffee, sugar, flour, etc.), we write it on the white board, and I eventually transfer the list to my shopping notebook that I take with me when I go shopping.

It's also a good idea to only shop once a week/month, that way you'll be less tempted by other things you see because you won't see them as often.

To have a list, you need to know what you're going to make, plus a store of essential items.

Don't buy processed food. These items are always expensive. It's far cheaper (and healthier) to make your own meals from fresh ingredients. If you're stuck for ideas, the internet is flooded with recipes.

If you have a few ingredients, but don't know what to make, simply type them into the search bar on Google (or another search engine) separated by a comma. For example, if you have an onion, some celery, and a carrot, type in "Onion, Celery, Carrot," hit enter, and it will return a list of recipes with those ingredients.

The best recipes are those that have few ingredients, are simple to make, and make enough for more than one meal, like lasagna, chilli, casserole, shepherd's pie, pasta.

What I do before I go shopping is look online at the weekly specials of the stores I'm going to. I make a note of all the specials of the items I usually buy, and I especially look for half-price specials.

I buy them while they're reduced and if I don't currently need them, I put them in my "spares" cupboard which is where I stockpile them until needed.

The caveat on doing this is to only buy things I normally use, and that have a long shelf life like mayonnaise, canned goods, washing powder and sauces.

It's funny that my husband used to smile and raise his eyes to heaven whenever he saw my stockpile of goods. But when the COVID restrictions and lockdowns happened in 2020, we were both grateful for everything I'd accumulated in the "spares" cupboard in the kitchen, along with all the washing powder, etc. that I'd accumulated in the laundry cupboard, and all the toothpaste, shampoo and other things that I'd been buying half-price and storing in the bathroom. It was nearly two months before we shopped again, preferring to stay home and away from the madness.

Having a stockpile also helps in case of illness or injury, or extreme weather conditions, which sometimes happens here in Australia, with sudden cyclones and other tropical storms and floods.

My Frugal Friend.

I learned a lot about being frugal from a friend I met over 20 years ago. She and her husband had a daughter and they lived in a three-bedroom house in the same town as me, and they were the most frugal people I'd ever met, and she taught me a lot about eating cheaply and eating well.

She was always telling me stories about things she'd done to save money and I was fascinated by them all.

One story I remember was that she and her husband had met while he was in the army. They married and lived in army accommodation.

They wanted to leave but didn't have enough money. He had nearly two more years to serve in the army, so they decided to not spend any money during that time so that they'd be able to buy a cheap house of their own.

And save they did. They didn't spend anything unless it was necessary, so no new clothes, no going out, no takeaways, no nothing.

She told me that during that time she wanted a coffee table but couldn't buy one. So, she collected cardboard tubes from toilet rolls, some flat cardboard from some empty boxes, and paper macheted a coffee table and painted it with some left-over paint and varnish that someone gave to her. She said it wasn't a great table, but it served its purpose at the time. I had to smile at her ingenuity.

She also told me that one time her husband had to go away on a training exercise for a month, so she bought some flour, margarine and vegetables and made 30 vegetable pasties and ate one every night for dinner while he was away. She said it was such a cheap month for groceries.

During the time I knew her, nothing had changed much with her. When it came to money, she really didn't like spending it. The house they lived in was a town house and they'd bought it with the money they'd saved when her husband was in the army. It was only a small house, but they made it work for them. And she still made cheap meals from vegetables.

It was also around the time of knowing my frugal friend and spending time with her that something else inspired me to see just how cheap, simple and filling meals could be. It was an advertisement on TV for cheese. The ad showed an old lady walking down the street carrying a wicker shopping basket over her arm. A large tipper truck full of potatoes suddenly roared past making her jump. But as it went by, a large potato fell from it and rolled back down the street to her feet.

She looked down at the potato, then looked directly into the camera and smiled knowingly.

The next shot was of the woman sitting at home at her kitchen table with the steaming, baked potato on a plate in front of her, split open and filled with grated cheese. She smiled knowingly at the camera again and picked up her knife and fork.

I watched it and thought how genius it was. Something as cheap and humble as a potato can be transformed so easily into a filling meal. It showed that meals don't need to be fancy or fussy to make. A baked potato can be a meal on its own, or a filling accompaniment to other things like stews, baked beans, vegetables and sauce, salad, and so much more.

One Pot Meals

Meals that only take one pot to cook them in are usually cheapest and can always be served with potato or bread or something else if you want to bulk it up.

Rice is cheap and can be cooked in one pot along with vegetables, beans, spices, tomatoes, and other ingredients. There are so many different rice dishes you can make.

Curry can be made in one pot too.

Simple things like potato, onion and capsicum can be slow cooked together and are delicious just on their own.

Pasta dishes are another one pot meal when added to mince, vegetables, a good sauce or some spices.

I have a large cast iron pan called a French pan, or sometimes it's known as a Dutch oven.

It's a heavy, cast iron, flat pan with a handle on either side and a lid. It can be used in the oven, but I've only ever used it on the stove top. It's works like a slow cooker, and I've made so many meals in it, and because it's so big, whatever I make there's always plenty left over for another meal for two, or it can make enough for a family of six.

I could go on and tell you even more ways to save money in the kitchen, but you can easily discover so much more once you start looking.

You've probably noticed that I don't mention meat. As I've said before, it's too expensive, I think it's incredibly unhealthy, it's an unnecessary 'food' item, and it causes so much distress, pain and suffering to the animals.

I used to believe the 'farmers love their animals' story, until I started looking into it, and everything I saw and read, showed the complete opposite.

Also, I think that there is something creepy about eating a corpse. We use the word 'meat' because it sounds more acceptable than saying 'dead animal.'

I wouldn't eat a dog or a cat, and I wouldn't eat a pig or a cow either. I don't hurt animals, nor do I pay others to hurt them for me.

As Paul McCartney once said. "If slaughter-houses had glass walls, we'd all be vegetarian." You can see the video of what he's talking about on YouTube. It's called Glass Walls and shows you what's inside the 'meat' industry. It shows what is being hidden from you, and what you will always hide from your children.

And if slaughterhouses and animals being cruelly confined in factory 'farms' isn't enough, the financial cost of supporting it is extremely high.

It's far better to cut 'meat' out of your diet as much as you can to save money and to save the animals.

I find a plant-based diet to be so much more varied than the old-style 'meat and two veg' meals. No sensible person eats like that anymore, especially when there are so many delicious meat-free, and extremely frugal ways to eat now.

Cutting back on your grocery bill is one of the biggest differences you can make to your budget, and it is completely in your control.

It's also one of the most interesting ways to save money because you'll find so many interesting meals to make that you probably never thought of before.

Chapter 7.
Understanding Your Electric Bill

The one thing we all use the most at home, without even realising it, is electricity. It's that invisible thing that works 24/7 and racks up a bill without us even realising it.

Once you start thinking about it, you'll see how many times you keep wasting it. But if you follow the advice in this chapter, you should be able to reduce your electric bill by up to 50%. Or more.

It starts by understanding your electricity bill and knowing how much each of your appliances are costing you to run.

Understanding Your Bill

Electricity is charged by the Kilowatt hour. On your bill it's written as kwh.

The word Kilo means 1,000 which is why there's 1,000 grams in a kilogram, 1,000 litres in a kilolitre, and 1,000 metres in a kilometre. Likewise, there's 1,000 watts in a kilowatt.

Electricity company's charge by the kilowatt hour. This means you pay for every 1,000 watts used in an hour.

Your bill will tell you how much you pay for each 1,000 watts used in an hour which won't be a lot, but it can add up quickly.

For example, right now in Australia electricity costs around 30c/kwh, which means that if I run an appliance that uses 1,000 watts, every hour I use it, it will cost 30c. So, if I run it for an hour, it will use 1,000 watts and it will cost me 30c. But if I only run it for half an hour, it will cost me 15 cents.

That doesn't sound like a lot of money, but if I was to use it for 30 mins a day for a month, that 15 cents becomes $4.50. And that's only for one appliance.

When you look at what your appliances cost to run, you'll quickly see that air conditioning is the most expensive to run, seconded by anything that heats up, like an oven, a hairdryer, a heater, hot water heater, a tumble dryer, stove top, electric pans, toaster and even electric blankets.

Appliances usually tell you about their wattage in the instruction manual, on a label on their electric cord, or printed on the bottom of them.

Something big like an air-conditioning unit can take 7 kilowatts an hour to run which is why the advice is always to not turn it on until you really need to, and if you do use it, turn it as low as you can.

7 kilowatts an hour at 30c/kwh will cost $2.10 an hour to run it. That may not sound a lot, but you'll probably run it for 10 hours a day in summer, which is $21 a day. Multiply that by 30 days a month and that's a whopping $630 a month, just to keep cool.

Turning it off for just one extra hour a day would save you $63 a month.

The good news that the wattage declared on appliances is the maximum. So, running it less than full blast will use less electricity and cost you less.

A portable room heater us usually around 2 kilowatts, so warming up just one room with a small portable heater can cost you $180 a month if you used it for 10 hours a day every day. And in winter, it's more likely that you'd use it for much more than 10 hours. If you get up at 7am and go to bed at 10pm, that 15 hours of non-stop heating every day.

So, look at your appliances and see how much they're costing you, and remember, every second they're on, they're costing you money. So don't leave lights on in empty rooms. Don't leave TV's on standby, and turn off your computer when you've finished it.

Turning things off, and turning things down are just two of the ways to reduce your electricity bill.

Here are several more.

Batch Cooking

Every time you turn your oven on it costs a lot of electricity to heat it up. So, turn it on once and make many things in it. For instance, make a casserole and make baked potatoes to go with it at the same time. Make a pasta bake, roast potatoes, and garlic bread all in one oven. Batch bake cookies, cake, pasties, and muffins.

If it's winter, having the oven on will help heat the house at the same time.

Regular Cleaning

Believe it or not, regular cleaning saves on electricity. You won't need to vacuum as long if the floors and carpets aren't as dirty. You won't need copious buckets of hot water for cleaning because nothing will be THAT dirty.

Microfibre cloths make cleaning easier, last well, so save time and money.

Windows

If it's really hot or really cold outside, close your windows to keep the heat out, or keep it in.

In summer, if it's hot outside, close your windows to help keep the house cooler. If the house does heat up during the day, you can open the windows at night to let the cooler air in.

I winter, keep the windows closed to keep the cold out. Just remember that when it's really cold, keep at least one window open a crack to let the condensation out so that mold doesn't develop. I you find that one of your walls gets damp a lot in winter, that is where your house is coldest and so it attracts condensation. That's where you should crack open a window so that the dampness has somewhere else to go.

In winter, if my windows are open during the day, I close them by 4pm because that's when the temperature drops, so I close up the house at that time to maintain the warmth.

Curtains

Curtains at windows don't just look nice and give you privacy, they can also help you to reduce your electric bill. In summer, keep them closed on sunny windows. Glass can heat up on a hot day, sometimes to the point of burning your skin if you touch it. Keeping the curtain closed traps the heat behind it which helps keep the room cool. Even thin cotton curtains can help.

When it's cold, closing curtains helps keep the house warm, especially at night when the temperature drops. I close my curtains as soon as it gets dark in winter so that the heating doesn't have to work as hard to keep the house warm.

Curtains trap the cold behind them in winter the same way they trap the heat in summer.

Doing The Laundry

There are two ways you can save money when you use your washing machine.

Firstly, only wash full loads. Doing small loads takes almost as much electricity as doing full loads, and you do twice as many. So, wait till you have enough dirty clothes to do a full wash.

Secondly, don't use hot water. Most things can be cleaned in cold water. I only use hot water for my sheets and towels. Everything else I wash in cold water. I once read that doing mostly cold water washes saves $230 a year, so I've been doing it ever since.

It's also money-saving to have both cold and hot water taps connected to your washing machine. It's far more economical to feed hot water into the machine than to feed in cold water and let the machine heat it itself.

Also, front loading machines need far less water than top loaders so that's a saving on hot water too. And, IMHO, the bumping action of the paddles in the rotating drum are more efficient at washing clothes, than the big upright paddle in a top loader that only swishes the clothes one way, then the other.

I find the front loaders to be cheaper to run and get the clothes cleaner, plus I don't have to bend myself double to reach the clothes in the bottom of an upright drum.

Showering

We all know that showering uses a lot less water than having a bath. But you can go even further than that.

In the early part of the 2,000's, here in Queensland Australia, we had an ongoing drought that lasted nearly eight years, getting progressively worse each year.

The government put many water restrictions in place, including sending every householder a 4-minute, waterproof egg-timer to stick on the shower wall, together with a huge TV advertising campaign, to get us to reduce our daily showering time to just 4 minutes. They even encouraged us to shower over a bucket and use the water that collected in it to water the garden. And it worked. We all reduced our shower-time to only 4 minutes, which is just enough time to wash hair and body and rinse off.

Someone told me that a 12-litre bucket took 4 minutes to fill. Most buckets are only 9 litres, but the hardware store sold 12 litre square buckets.

So, I bought a couple and we used them to shower over. I remember keeping a constant eye on the bucket, knowing that as soon as it was full, I had to turn off the shower. When I carried my bucket out into the dry, parched garden, it seemed like just a small drop of water compared to what the garden really needed.

The 4-miniute shower routines lasted for a couple of years at the time, and it's a habit that's stayed with me. My showering time may be a bit longer than

4 minutes now, but they are still "no nonsense" showers. I get in, get on with what I have to do, then get out.

This saves me both time and money.

Hot Water Instantly

I've lived in quite a few different places throughout my life and had different hot water systems – instant gas hot water, instant electric hot water, and electric hot water tank.

It's always the instant hot water systems that are the most efficient because they heat the water straight away as soon as you turn on the tap. Water coming from an electric hot water tank always seems to take longer because it first feeds cold water through which mingles with the hot water as it comes through which leaves me waiting for the water to get hot enough to use.

The cost of electricity between the two systems can be huge over time. Look at it this way, When I want to fill a bucket with hot water, if the water is coming from a hot water tank, I run the water till it comes through hot, then I fill the bucket. If it's coming from an instant hot water heater, I put the bucket straight under the hot tap, and turn it off when the bucket is full. That is so much more efficient.

An instant hot water heater only needs to heat the water you use. A hot water tank heats the whole tank of water every day whether you use it or not. So even when you're away on holiday, your electric hot water system will reheat the tank every day.

According to the Australian Government Department of Industry, Science, Energy and Resources, "Instant hot water systems use 30% of energy that a hot water tank uses." This means instant hot water systems are 70% cheaper to run.

When you need to renew your hot water system, take a good look at the running costs between instant hot water systems and hot water tanks.

Dish Washers

Some people love dish washers, some people don't like them, while others find them useful sometimes but not always.

I'm in the latter category. I have a dishwasher drawer because it came with the apartment, but I don't use it a lot.

But love them or not, there's several financial considerations you need to make when it comes to using a dishwasher.

Firstly, it can ruin your dishes. One of the major complaints I hear from people who use their dishwashers often is that their glasses go 'cloudy' and their crockery looks 'scratched.' This increases the cost of replacing these items repeatedly.

Secondly, dishwashers are not always efficient because things don't always get cleaned properly or something blocks the arms from turning or items weren't stacked properly. This results in having to do another cycle or washing everything by hand. Again, this costs money to have to re-do what should have been done correctly in the first place.

Thirdly is the cost of the dishwasher tablets. These aren't cheap and cost several hundred dollars a year to buy. Compare that to the cost of handwashing liquid which is less than $50 a year.

Fourthly, there's the running cost of each load. Dishwashers heat the water to a much higher temperature than tap water. There's also the cost of electricity to run each cycle which takes 2-3 hours every time.

Fifthly, and this is the biggest cost of all, is the money to buy a dishwasher which is several hundred dollars to thousands $$. And you'll probably have to pay for delivery and installation too. By comparison, a washing up bowl and drying rack, will probably cost $20-$50.

When you compare the two ways of washing dishes, hand washing can save you thousands of dollars.

People often complain that handwashing dishes takes too long, but I disagree. I look at it this way; regardless of how you wash your dishes, they still need rinsing first, so no time is saved there.

Stacking the dishwasher takes time depending on how many dishes you have. Also, the kitchen countertops need wiping once the dishes are in the dishwasher. When the dishwasher is finished, you have to take everything out and put it away, and some things will have pools of water on top that you'll have to wipe. Then finally the dishwasher itself needs to be wiped out.

If you wash the dishes by hand, once they're rinsed and the bowl is full of hot soapy water, it takes about 20 minutes to wash, wipe, put away and wipe the counter tops. The best part is, everything is done, and you don't have to go back later and start unloading, wiping, and putting away.

Plus, I always find that standing over a bowl of hot soapy water, wiping dishes, is quite therapeutic.

Early To Bed

Going to bed early can save you a lot of money when it's so hot you're running air conditioning, or it's so cold you have the heating on.

I always think that the bedroom is not a good room to run air conditioning when I'm sleeping. Recycled air is not healthy. It's far better to use a fan and sleep under nothing but a cotton sheet.

Likewise, it's not good to sleep in a heated room. Blankest and pyjamas can keep you warm at night.

Turning off the air-conditioning or heating and having an early night can be a real money saver.

People will often tell me that its 'impossible' to sleep without air-conditioning when it's hot. But I always remind them that people did it for thousands of years before air-conditioning was invented. And right now we're talking about ways to save money, not making up excuses to spend more money.

If you're sat on the couch at night driving up your electric bill by the minute with the air-conditioning or heating running, think about turning it off and watching TV in bed. Or go to bed and read a book.

Just think about it like this; if you go to bed just one hour earlier, in a week that's seven hours of electricity saved. So, if your cooling/heating is costing just $2 an hour, in a month, you'll have saved $60.

That's a lot of money for no effort.

Get Out More

Going out more can reduce your electric bill, especially when it's really hot or really cold.

But no matter what time of year, going out saves you money because while you're out, you're not running up the electric bill at home.

When my kids were young, if it was hot in summer or cold in winter, I'd take them to the public library for a couple of hours and then we'd walk to the shops to get a few groceries or go to the park.

The kids loved to go out and I'd take advantage of the coolness or warmth of the library and the shopping mall. We'd take drinks with us so that I didn't need to buy any, and we'd all enjoy some out of the house time, which was free to do, and we weren't running up bills at home.

I remember one winter, I walked them to a grocery store that was a one hour walk away. At the back of the shops was a small park with a pond. I took a few crusts of bread with me, and we fed the ducks once we arrived after our one-hour walk. Then we went to the supermarket and bought the items on my list (they were at greatly reduced prices, hence my wish to go there) and then we walked home.

I felt that our afternoon out was a win-win-win-win. It was a nice walk, the kids enjoyed it, the ducks got fed, and I saved money.

I've always done as much as I can to reduce my electricity bill. None of it is hard to do and the savings can be huge.

Not long ago, I was reading a post on social media. A woman was asking for ways to reduce her electric bill, which she said was over a thousand dollars a quarter. I was astounded that her bill was so high. She also said that she and her husband both worked, so they weren't home much.

How she got her bill so high I have no idea. At the time, mine was between $300 and $350 a quarter, and I work from home, so I'm in more than I'm out.

I could only guess that it was probably because she turns on the heating as soon as it gets cold, whereas I put on a jumper.

Chapter 8.
Kids and Saving Money

One of the biggest drains on your money can be kids – but only if you let them. So, the trick is to not let them.

Kids are the world's master manipulators and usually know how to emotionally control their parents. The hardest thing for parents is to not fall for it, which is difficult because we always want our kids to be happy.

But sometimes it's okay to say no to them. In fact, letting them know that they can't have everything they want in life is a good lesson to teach them. It's also okay if they don't have the latest electronic gadget, even if "all my friends have got one."

The Young Ones

When kids are young, especially when they're toddlers, they are much more easily entertained and are less materially demanding.

Young children only want to be with their parents, so no matter what you do or where you go, they just want to be with you.

I used to take my kids out for walks a lot when they were young and take them to the library or to the park and push them on the swings. These things are free, and they loved it.

I also used to take them to the local church coffee mornings and local school fetes. These things were incredibly cheap, and the kids enjoyed it.

They'd sit happily eating biscuits in the church hall and watching everything going on at the fete.

Buying them clothes was easy. Kids grow quickly, so the charity stores were full of hardly worn kids' clothes that were incredibly cheap. So, I'd buy things that fit them now, would fit them soon, and would fit them one day. That way, I had a whole stash of clothes waiting whenever they went through a growth spurt, and at that age they seemed to be constantly growing. The bonus at that young age is that they don't care what they wear, so whatever I bought they would wear without protest.

Older Kids

Raising children becomes more expensive as they get older. Young children don't care if they have the latest smart phone, or the best computer. They just want to have fun, so are happy with just a few toys and to watch a few kids' shows on TV.

Older kids, from pre-puberty to older teens seem to be unhappy unless they get everything they want. Sadly, most of their wants are material, although some still want their parent's attention.

All children are different, but the most important thing to remember is to not let them rule you with their demands on your time and money. I've always found that saying no to them helps with discipline when they realise that they can't have things just because they want them.

Here is my list of just some of the ways you can save your sanity and your money when it comes to children.

School Lunch

It won't hurt them one bit to take a packed lunch to school every day, and it can also save you thousands of dollars every year. It also saves a lot of time if you get your kids to pack their own lunch every day. Doing things for themselves is a good life lesson. Just make sure you have plenty of cheap snacks and drinks ready for them to take.

Free Entertainment

There are plenty of ways to keep the kids entertained for free, like a day at the beach, a drive to the country, after school and school holiday free activities, time at the local library where they can use the computers for free, play games and borrow books, music, movies, and toys.

Picnics on a day out are free and you can pack sandwiches and snacks, or buy hot chips to share which will only set you back $5 or so.

Clothes

This is something you should budget for so that you always have money to buy them new clothes, or if they're older and want to pick their own stuff, they know the limit of what they can spend.

Hand-me-downs from an older sibling to a younger one is great too. It means the younger child gets more clothes from what's donated as well as what's bought from their clothing budget. Donated items from friends' kids are okay too.

If the older kids are choosing their own things, just make sure they're not forgetting to buy things they need like underwear and shoes.

Saying No

It's important to say no to your kids about things they shouldn't be doing, or that may be physically dangerous. It's also okay to say no to other demands as well.

Kids don't need to have the latest electronic gadget. They don't need to be taken to McDonalds just because they suddenly feel like going. And you don't have to drop everything you're doing because they suddenly decide to go hang out with a friend and they need you to drive them there NOW!

Teenagers are the worst offenders for making on the spot demands for a ride to the mall, or to go somewhere with their friend, or to let their friend sleepover, even though it's late and you were looking forward to a quiet night in.

I was once given advice about how to deal with sudden demands from teenagers asking for an immediate response, and its gold. It worked every time. And it's this:

If a teenager wants to suddenly do something or go somewhere and they're demanding to know straight away if they can do it or not and they're rushing you to make an immediate decision, just say, "I'm not sure. Leave it with me and I'll think about it. but if you want an answer right now, then the answer is no."

If they keep on insisting on an answer, just repeat it again and say "unless you give me time to think about it, the answers no. But it's up to you."

This forces them to make the decision, not you. If they try and say something like, their friend is asking them to go somewhere and their parents are giving them a lift straight away so it's now or never, say it's never.

This puts an end to their constant manipulation, plus it quickly teaches them to never pressure you into an on-the-spot response, because they already know what it's going to be.

Electronics

All kids have electronics, whether it's a mobile phone, iPad, laptop, or desktop computer. If you have several kids, it can get extremely expensive to keep buying these things.

The only way to make it easier is to budget for them. Most electronics have a useable life span of only 3 years, although sometimes it can be longer, but eventually most things become too old to update.

But knowing that there is a minimum 3-year window before things need to be replaced lets you make an educated guess at how much you need to set aside each month to make it happen.

Don't fall into the trap of buy-now-pay-later schemes. You don't want to be paying for something that will quickly be worth less than you'll eventually pay for it. If you fall on financial hard times and want to sell the item to pay the debt off, you'll find that even after just a week or two of owning it, it can be worth as little as 50% of what you bought it for.

If you save regularly and pay it outright, you'll not only have no debt hanging over you for years, but if you need to sell it, the money you get is yours.

But kids don't need extremely expensive electronic items. They just need to have ones that are fit for the purpose they're using them.

So don't worry about it. Your kids will be fine.

Pocket Money

All kids should have pocket money, but they don't need to be rich. No matter how much or how little you give them, they'll always think that it's not enough, so don't feel bad.

Kids get all their needs taken care of, so their pocket money is for frivolous or unnecessary things, so large amounts of money aren't necessary.

When I was a kid, my parents gave me pocket money each week, and 'present' money which I had to keep in a jar in my bedroom and use it for buying gifts for people for birthdays and Christmas.

My parents were always stingy with money, so my pocket money and present money were extremely low amounts. My parents never, not once, gave me lunch money for school, never bought me an ice-cream when we were having a day out, smacked me if I ever asked them to buy me something when we were in a shop, and I was not allowed to have anything to eat in between meals, even though they sat at the dining room table and had tea and biscuits every afternoon.

They said that being so restrictive with money would teach me a good lesson about the value of money. They were wrong. All it taught me was how stingy and mean my parents were.

There's nothing wrong with a hot school meal now and again, or the odd ice-cream on a warm day out.

But apart from that, if kids want more, well that is what their pocket money is for.

Pets

One thing that is a bad idea for so many reasons is buying a pet for a child. Liking animals is great, but it's still no reason to own one, and kids get bored with things quickly, and a pet is a long-term commitment. That's why buying a child a pet is a complete no-no.

And it's for more than the cruelty aspect of a long-suffering, neglected animal. There is also a huge financial cost.

A child cannot be expected to pay for all the ongoing expenses of pet ownership like food, bedding, and vet fees. Any animal, no matter how small costs money. Even a mouse needs a cage, bedding, and regular cleaning out. Dogs and cats require oh so much more, plus they can live for up to 20 years or more.

I've known plenty of people who bought pets for their children, and they all eventually regretted it. Some of the kids grew bored with their new responsibility within a couple of weeks. Even those who bought pets for their teenagers claiming that the kids would take the dog/cat with them when they moved out, were wrong. They all (every single one of them) ended up keeping it.

But as I already said, pets are expensive and sometimes those expenses come without warning. So even if you yourself are contemplating getting a furry companion, my advice, for financial reasons, is don't do it. Unless, of course, you are 100% committed to having a dog or cat because they fill you with joy and your income allows it.

Holidays/Eating out

Both can be expensive, but they don't need to be.

Holidays are something you should budget for. This is easy to do. You look at how much it would cost you to take the family away on vacation for a week or two. Browse a few brochures or do an online search.

It's best to go somewhere that your kids will enjoy, but it doesn't have to be much. Just a cheap motel with a pool can be entertainment enough.

I knew a woman who owns a small caravan. It has one bedroom, plus bunk beds and the table folds down into another bed too. She has three kids.

Every school holiday, she and her husband tow the caravan to a caravan park and drive their second car there too. She stays a week or two with the boys while her husband goes home during the weekdays because he must go to work.

She swears by these cheap holidays. They take the kids bikes with them and stay at large parks with swings, a pool, a jumping pillow, and plenty of paths for the kids to ride around.

They cook their own meals while they're away and maybe go out for pizza one night and perhaps go ten-pin bowling. But the rest of the time the boys ride their bikes and hang out with all the other kids and swim, and at night they all watch movies together and eat popcorn. It's always a cruisy holiday for them and because it's so cheap, they do it during every school term break.

Holidays with the kids, no matter where you go, are always better if you stay somewhere that has a kitchen, so that you don't have to eat out all the time. Plus, it's easier to make the kids something they like than to try and pick something from a restaurant menu that they may not like. Kids are usually happy with simple food.

Once you do a search to see what a holiday will cost you, you can then figure out how much to save each month, but don't forget to include spending money while you're there which can sometimes cost more than the holiday itself, unless you're smart.

If you get stuck in just a hotel room with nothing more than a kettle, if you have food flasks with you, you can make instant oats, instant soup, and instant noodles. Combine any of those with a ready-made salad, or a bread roll, or a ready-made sandwich, and you've got yourself a half-decent meal.

These things can be packed and eaten on a day out. We've often pout dried noodles and instant soup mix in a food flask and poured in boiling water. We take it with us when we go out, along with a fork each, and at lunch time we sit in the park and enjoy our food. Instant noodles are delicious when cooked in the soup.

One day we took a homemade pizza with us for a picnic. It was still on the metal pizza plate it had cooked on earlier that day. I sliced it and covered it in foil, and we took it with us along with a packet of corn chips and some fruit.

It was late afternoon when we arrived at the beach for our impromptu picnic, and I left the pizza on the car dashboard in the sun.

We went for a walk for about an hour and ate our food at a picnic table in the park by the beach while we watched the sun go down, and the pizza had reheated nicely.

Taking sandwiches to eat and buying hot chips to go with it has always been a firm favourite of ours, because it's a compromise between eating our own food and eating out. And somehow hot chips always go well with a sandwich,

Sunny days are great for warming food in the car when we're out. If there is no sun, then food flasks are a great fall back. We've even put cooked sausages and fried onions into a warmed-up food flask and eaten hot dogs on a picnic. I'd even brought ketchup and mustard in tiny plastic containers, and a knife to spread them on the hot dog rolls.

It's amazing what you can come up with when you get creative.

If you want to go somewhere expensive, like a theme park, have look online and see if you can find out what food is available there so that you have a better idea what it will cost you and what the best choice is for you and your family.

Expensive days out are best kept as treats rather than the norm, because the kids get high expectations, and the cost can be ridiculous.

Another money-saving piece of advice is, whenever you eat out, even if it's food from the fish and chip shop to take to the park, bring your own drinks. The cost of buying a drink, even a 'cheap' soft drink, can cost almost the same as the food.

Chapter 9.
Cost Per Use

This is by far one of the greatest money-making decisions you can make, and that is, figuring out how much something will cost you every time you use it.

Cost Per Use

When we buy something, we tend to only think of the quality of what we're buying and trying to figure out if it's worth the price we're paying.

A better, and more cost-effective way is looking at cost-per-use.

Let me explain it this way. Say you want to buy a nice outfit for going out to restaurants and parties, and say the one you want to buy is $100, but you think it's worth it because it looks really fancy.

But then you think about how often you'd wear it, which would be maybe two or three times a year when you go for a meal on your birthday, your wedding anniversary, plus if you get invited to a party (which happens once every two or three years) you could wear it then too.

This means that if you wear the outfit three times in one year, it will cost you $33.33 per use/wear.

But if you bought a less fancy outfit for $60, it would cost you $20 per use/wear over the next year.

But, I hear you say, you'll probably keep it for at least a couple of years, in which case it will cost you $17 per use for the $100 outfit or $10 for the $60 outfit. It's still a high price per use.

At the same time, you might be looking at a T-shirt you want to buy that costs $20. You think that's a lot for one T-shirt. But thinking about how much you'd wear it, you'd probably wear it at least once a week or two, which would be at least 25 times a year, so the cost per use would be 80c. But I hear you argue, it would only last one year if you wore it that much so you'd have to buy another, which will increase the cost of purchase to $40 and cost per use to $1.60.

That's still far cheaper than the fancy outfits that cost $17 and $10 per use.

This same principle applies to everything you buy. I find that stopping to consider cost per use before I buy things stops me from buying things I don't really need once I realise how few times I'd wear it or use it.

I know someone who bought a toasted sandwich maker a year ago. He said it was a bargain at $50 because he loves toasted sandwiches.

So far, he's only used it once and that was the same day he bought it.

Looking at the cost per use, that must be the world's most expensive toasted sandwich that he ate. I hope it was worth it.

Three years ago, I bought an air-fryer. I'd never had one before, nor did I know anyone else who had one. So why did I want one? For two reasons. The first is that it takes little to no oil to fry food in an air-fryer. Secondly, they cook things faster and in a smaller space, making it a big saving in electricity.

I did some online research to find out what else could be cooked in an air-fryer beside chips. It turned out that different air-fryers had different capabilities from cheap ones that could only fry food, to more expensive models that could be used for making cake and bread.

So, I bought a more expensive model at $500 which seemed a bit obsessive, but I figured that on the electricity it would save, it would pay for itself in no time.

And I was right. Everything is so economical to make if I use the air-fryer, and I can even make cakes in it, plus baked potatoes, hot chips, spring rolls, roast potatoes, and it even reheats food well too. It turns out, an air-fryer is more like a small oven, so it can cook a lot of things, and do it in a fraction of the time and cost.

I look at it this way, it's a lot cheaper to cook freezer food in the air-fryer for 10 minutes than to heat up the oven and run it for 20 minutes. The air-fryer works from cold because it heats up in seconds.

And over the 3 years I've had it, I use it every week, often several times a week. I reckon I easily average using it 3 times per week, which is over 150 times a year. Over the 3 years since I bought it, that 450 times, which works out at just over $1 per use, and that will get cheaper over time, plus it's already paid for itself in the saving of electricity, and it's saved me a lot of time too.

But I did my research before I bought the air-fryer to make sure that I would use it a lot. The things I was looking for were things that I already make. It's no good buying an appliance that is only good at making things I never eat. That's why the air-fryer was a good fit for me because it allows me to make things that I regularly make in half the time it usually takes, with less than half the fat, and uses much less electricity than a regular-sized oven.

Another bonus is that when I move (and I've done so twice in the past year), I take it with me and keep using it.

Cutting The Cost at Source.

Another way to cut down on cost-per-use is to not pay as much for something in the first place.

I always buy electric appliances (and beds) new so that they come with a guarantee, and I know that no-one has misused it.

Other things I'm happy to buy used if they're still in good condition. I fact my desk that I'm sitting at right now is one that I bought from a charity shop five years ago. It cost me $235 plus $30 delivery charge, but it was well worth it because I use it every single day, sometimes for up to 12-15 hours at a time, and it has 8 deep drawers which are perfect for holding all my writing gear.

Over the 5 years since I bought it, I've used it over 1,800 times and probably for about 15,000 hours altogether. Looking at cost-per-use, it has so far cost me 14 cents a day to use my desk.

Compare that to around $500 to $800 a month that companies charge per month to rent a desk in a commercial office, and it's a huge saving.

Plus, I intend to go on using my desk for many more years.

And all that's not even factoring in all the money I've earned while sitting at my desk. Writing is how I earn a living, so to me, this desk is priceless.

But getting back to the subject of buying things second-hand, it's a way to reduce CPU (Cost-Per-Use) at the source because used goods are usually cheaper to buy than new goods.

But don't go browsing for used goods unless there's something you're particularly looking for, otherwise you'll end up buying a load of junk you don't need.

Charity stores are good places to find bargains as well as pawnshops, Facebook Marketplace, and garage sales. Secondhand markets are handy too.

A few years ago, I wanted a new table and chairs set for my veranda. All I had was an old bistro set that had seen better days and wasn't going to last much longer. I went to a nearby garage sale and saw a small table and four chairs. The tops were wooden, and the legs were metal. After a quick inspection, it seemed to be in great condition, but it needed of a bit of cosmetic TLC. It was priced at $60. I spoke to the woman selling it and said, "Will you take $50 for the table and chairs." She immediately said, "Done."

I carried them home, piece by piece (I didn't have the car with me), used them for a few weeks, then bought some sandpaper, a small can of wood varnish and metal paint, and set to work.

I just 3 days I had a beautiful table and 4 chair setting that looked great on the veranda. Since moving, it now looks just as great on my balcony. And all for $80, and it will last for years.

Buying used items is a real money-saver, but only if you choose wisely. Don't buy something just because it's cheap. Cheap doesn't mean you want it or need it. You might see something that only costs $1. That may seem like a bargain, but what you must ask yourself is would you want it if it was $5 or $10? If it starts to look less interesting at a higher price, it's probably because you don't really want it.

But if it's something that you're looking for and it's at a reduced price, then it probably is a true bargain. Just don't forget to figure out what the CPU will be, which depends on how often you plan to use it or wear it.

I even do the same with food items. When I'm shopping for groceries, I always think about what I'm going to make with something before I buy it. So, for instance, if it's a cabbage, I think of what I'm going to make with it, (stir-fry, spring rolls, chow main, etc.), how many meals I'll get out of it, and how much per serving.

With the cabbage, by adding a few other vegetables and some rice, I can probably make several meals that cost only $1 per head. On the other hand, if I buy a ready-made family pie for $10, that's $2.50 per head, plus all the potatoes and vegetables to go with it, which adds up to a lot more per head.

It doesn't take long for savings like this to add up. Just $1 saved every day is $365 a year.

And when you factor in CPU with everything you buy, the savings can be huge.

My advice is to not buy anything unless you get so much use out of it, the CPU comes down to $0 or there abouts.

Chapter 10.
Retail and Resale

Whenever you buy something from a store the cost is called the retail price, because you've bought it from a retailer, which is someone, or a company, that sells things to customers. Retailers buy their products from wholesalers and sell them on to you for a profit. That's business.

The customer (you) however, cannot sell the item you bought for a profit because as soon as you buy something, it's value decreases because it's no longer new. And this is what we're going to talk about in this chapter; the difference in retail and resale

There is a book I've read several times, The Millionaire Next Door (see a link to this book on the last page.)

This book is all about the difference between perceived millionaires, and actual millionaires. The researcher who wrote the book went looking for millionaires to interview in upmarket neighborhoods where everyone had big houses and expensive cars, and some had boats and jet skis.

But instead of millionaires, all they found were people drowning in debt to pay for all the things they couldn't afford, like big houses, expensive cars, boats, and jet skis. It turned out that not only did they not own these items, but they were living pay-day to pay-day and if they were ever out of work with no income for just a couple of months, they'd lose everything.

Instead, they found the real millionaires living in normal houses, living unassuming lives, with no debt, and years of savings in the bank.

The most surprising thing was that most of the unassuming millionaires were earning just as much money as the fake millionaires. The only difference was what they did with their money. They bought modest houses, lived modest lives, had no credit card debt, and if they were to lose their jobs, they had enough money in savings to last them several years.

One of the things that I found most interesting (as well as the part about they still clipped coupons) was that before they bought anything, they would consider how much they could get for it if they had to resell it. They thought it was pointless to have a house full of hundreds of thousands of possessions, that were only worth a few thousand if they needed to sell them.

Not only did they only buy things that provided value to their lives, but they considered the value of it once they'd bought it.

It turned out that auctioneers were the people that mostly considered the resale value of everything they bought, because they'd often seen the heartbreak of people who were drowning in debt, being forced into bankruptcy, and crying as strangers paid a few dollars at auction for their possessions that they'd treasured for years and bought at high prices that they couldn't afford.

This is why it's important to consider the resale value of everything you buy, including your clothes. Clothing can be expensive to buy, but just remember that even if you never wear it and it still has the price tag on it, it's worth either very little, or nothing. I'm guessing everything in your wardrobe is worth nothing. It's the same for everyone, that's why unwanted clothing is always donated to charity stores, because no one will buy it privately.

I see online that people try and resell the expensive prom dress they bought for their daughter. Some of these dresses were bought for $3,000. And I always wonder why anyone would pay so much for a child to attend one unimportant event. Did the outfit make sure they had a better time? Of course not and buying it in the first place is why the parents aren't millionaires. That's why they're desperately trying to sell it online for just a few hundred dollars. And these listings stay up for weeks and months with no takers.

But it's not just prom dresses and general clothing that loses its value as soon as you buy it. Everything does.

Think about that next time the salesperson in the store is telling you that you can take home that expensive item right now for no money down and five years to pay it off. In five years' time you'll still be making payments on the full price of an item that's now worth far less than half of what you're paying for it.

Do you really want to be in that position?

Look around your home right now. Look at everything in your home – the couch, the TV, the fridge, etc. How much did you pay for them altogether?

Now think about how much you could sell them for if you were desperate for money. It's sobering to think how little they're worth.

The thing to do is stop buying things you don't need. And for the things you do need, buy them when they're cheaper on the stores like at the end of financial year sales, end of season sell-off, or when they're trying to shift their current stock to make room for the new stuff.

And never be afraid to haggle. If they're desperate to move stock out of their store (especially large items like couches, fridges, and tables) they are usually quite negotiable on price.

Just keep the resale value in mind.

Chapter 11.
Free Days Out

This is where we talk about saving money when you're not at home. And the best price to pay for a fun day out is $0.

But is this really possible?

Yes, it is.

The problem with where we live is that we rarely make the most of what we can do there.

Just recently someone was complaining to me that they were bored because they were broke, so they couldn't go anywhere. I did a quick google search and found that within walking distance from their home, there was a free museum and a forest walk that had trails suitable for wheelchairs (not that they have a wheelchair, but it means a flat, easy trail).

They were amazed and said they had no idea they lived near a museum or a forest walk.

And this goes to show that there may be free things to do where you live, but you just don't know.

These may even be one-off free events in your area that you haven't heard about. I'm on a local email list that always sends out a list of local things that are going on, both paid and free. There are also a few local groups where people get together and go for walks and picnics in the park.

But even if there's nothing much going on where you live, there are always things you can do that won't cost you anything.

Here is a list of things you can try.

Picnics. This is the obvious one. Choose a place to eat that's a fun walk to get to. Don't forget to pack a drink for each person. The bottles can be refilled with tap water. Take a few things to do like books, balls, or other outdoor games. If the thought of picnic food is boring, you can always buy some hot chips to go with it. Not free, but not expensive either.

Walks. This is another obvious free thing to do, but if you look on a local map, or do an online search, you'll probably find places to walk that you didn't even know about. On a map, look for green areas and go see what's there.

Swings. Young kids love to play on swings in the park. Find a park that has some and take them there, preferably one that's in walking distance. I used to take my son to a park with swings that was a one hour walk away, but he loved going there and we enjoyed walking there and back too. It was always a fun afternoon out.

Gardens. If you're lucky enough to have some botanical gardens nearby, they are a great place to walk around and relax. It's always interesting to read all the names of the plants too.

Public Libraries. This is an all-weather place to go. Libraries are not only free, but they often have more going on than you realise. You can not only borrow books, but also eBooks, audio books, movies, and music. Children can borrow toys, stay for story-time, and there are often free talks for adults too. They usually have free computers you can use, and board games you can play.

Beach. It's always nice to go to the beach just to hear the waves. I love laying on the warm sand and kids love digging in it. The sound of the ocean is always soothing and jumping in the waves is always fun. Getting rid of all the sand off your body and belongings afterwards is always entertaining too.

Galleries and Museums. Some galleries and museums you must pay to get into and some you don't. Do a search for free galleries and museums in your area.

Garden Fun. It's possible to spend an afternoon in your own garden. There are plenty of outdoor games to play and just kicking a ball around can be fun, or searching for four-leaf covers, or making daisy chains, or throwing a frisbee. My kids even liked to picnic in our own backyard. Strangely they thought the food tasted much better out there. And somehow, I had to agree. You can also get the kids to help you work in the garden or plant seeds in the veggie patch.

Google More to Do. If you want more things to do for free, do a Google search for what to do in your area or for upcoming free events. There's probably more going on where you live than you realise.

Failing everything else, just go for a walk. If you live near a city, go for a walk in the city. If you live in a town, go for a walk around your town, around streets where you usually never go. Go at different times of the day.

And if it's too wet to go out, stay in and read, watch a movie that everyone likes, do a jigsaw together, make cookies, play computer games, do crafts.

When you put your mind to it, there are so many things you can do for free.

And they're fun.

Chapter 12.
Gift Giving

Giving gifts can become so expensive that it physically hurts. It's money that you don't get the benefit of because you're buying stuff for other people. And it always seems that no matter how much you spend on others, you never seem to get as much in return.

But I don't know your family dynamics and how you do everything at certain holiday times, but I can tell you what I do, and it has worked really well.

Christmas

I believe that Christmas is for children, not adults. The only reason families get together at this time of year is because everyone has time off work, even if it's just one day.

Years ago, when I was a cash-poor single parent, I instructed everyone not to buy me gifts anymore and that I wouldn't be buying them any either. I also asked them not to send me Christmas cards either.

The first Christmas I said this, they all ignored me, and the gifts and cards still arrived, but I sent nothing to them.

Naturally they all tried to argue with me and used words like "tradition" and "season of good will" and all manner of rhetoric. But I stood my ground and said I respected their beliefs that gift-giving was an obligation, so they should respect my belief that it's not, and that forcing me to accept gifts when I had expressly asked them not to do so was bullying.

Eventually they all gave up the argument and agreed to leave me out of all the forced gift exchanging. I also said that if they did give me anything I'd donate it to the charity store and throw their cards in the bin. They couldn't believe that I didn't want a card, so I explained to them my reasons, of which I have three.

Firstly, so many trees must be cut down. People go on and on about protecting our planet, yet don't see a problem with forests being felled so that they can send a card to everyone they know.

Secondly, cards are pointless. Most people only want to give cards so they can receive them and hang them up to show off how many "friends" they have. It's simply virtue signaling, which is an ugly thing to do. Plus, we all put up cards then throw them all away. So, what's the point? What a waste of time. And trees.

Thirdly, everyone hates writing and sending cards at Christmas. Whenever you talk to someone about it, they always complain about how much time it took them to write out all the cards and then the time to deliver them by hand or mail them. Everyone I've ever met who gives out cards at Christmas, moans about doing it. So, I tell people that I don't want a card from them because I know they wrote it in anger, so I don't want their negativity.

I then tell them that they're wasting their time writing a card for me because I'll just throw it straight in the bin because I have no use for it, and it was written in anger.

Once I tell people my reasons for not wanting Christmas cards, they never disagree and will even admit that I'm "damn lucky" that I don't have to write and send cards.

I use the same argument with gifts and say that everyone hates Christmas shopping and that they always bitch and whine about it too.

Christmas day lunch is also pointless and causes stress to those who cook it and those who are obligated to go and eat it.

My family always got together on Christmas day. But once I stopped going, the get-togethers got shorter and shorter until they all stopped doing it at all. And you know what? They all seemed relieved and much happier.

When I was a kid, every Christmas Day we would spend the day at my parents' friends' house, along with another family.

The adults stayed in the kitchen/dining room all day and us kids were expected to all play together and have a great time.

I never understood why adults thought that throwing a bunch of kids together would mean they'd get along.

I hated those Christmas Days and was glad when we moved to another state and spent Christmas Day at home instead.

Before we moved, we'd get up early, open all our presents and then had to leave them all and go to the other house for a day and be bored out of our minds. And this visit wasn't just for a few hours. It spanned over lunch and dinner time, and then we'd be put to bed and woken up again, when it was late and we were going home. Ugh! We all hated it.

So, I knew that when I told my son we'd be staying home on Christmas day and not visiting the family, he'd love the idea. And he did. He also got to open his gifts from the family at the same time he opened his gifts from me instead of having to wait till he saw them later that day

I was much happier spending my gift-buying money on my son rather than on family who were a lot financially better off than me, and relatives that I rarely saw.

Instead, my son received plenty of gifts and we stayed home all day with the TV on, watching plenty of Christmas movies and grazing all day on the "party food" that I made the previous day, which was chips, dips, pasties, mini pizzas, and cocktail sausage rolls. What kid wouldn't enjoy a day like this?

The only others I bought gifts for were the children of relatives and close friends, because, like I said previously Christmas is for children, not adults. And every kid is happy to stay home on Christmas day and play with their gifts.

Birthdays

Again, this is where I believe that only children should be given gifts on their birthday, so that's what I do. I also give gifts to elderly relatives because they have been a part of birthday gift-giving all their lives and would be upset if I didn't give them anything, so for this reason I've always done it. Sadly, I'm now down to only one elderly relative. The rest have passed away over the years.

So now I only buy birthday gifts for children of immediate family members which are my own children, my grandchildren, and the children of my siblings (nieces and nephews.) But once the kids turn 18, that's their last birthday gift because they are officially adults and capable of going out to work and buying their own things.

Anniversaries

The only anniversary I bother with is my own wedding anniversary, because my marriage means a lot to me.

But my husband and I don't buy each other a gift. Instead, we buy something for our home that's frivolous, so we wouldn't normally buy it.

Over the years our frivolous anniversary gifts to ourselves have included an oil painting, cut crystal wine glasses, candle wall sconces, and a chiming clock. All these items weren't necessary, but we did want them, and I still enjoy having them all.

The last few years we've stopped buying anniversary gifts because we now have everything we want, and we don't want to fill our home with too many things.

So now we celebrate it by going out for a meal or sitting on the balcony eating a takeaway. Or we just stay in, drink wine (in our cut crystal wine glasses, of course), eat garlic bread, and talk and laugh a lot.

We never feel the need to throw a party or invite others to join us. Our anniversary is ours and ours alone, so we don't need other people.'

And to be honest, some years we forget it's our anniversary until a few days after the date. And then we laugh.

Annual Holidays

Christmas isn't the only time of year that people get together. There is Valentine's Day, Easter, New Year's Eve/Day, and depending on where you live in the world, there can be others, like Anzac Day in Australia, and Independence Day, Groundhog Day, and Thanksgiving in America.

I find annual holidays to be too much of an obligation, so I participate in none, because the truth is, whether you take part in these things or not, it doesn't matter. Nothing changes. Life goes on as usual.

And these annual holiday get-togethers are just one more thing that people complain about having to do. There is so much bad feeling if someone doesn't get the right gift, or doesn't get a gift, or if they don't want to spend all day travelling to see you.

Mother's Day is one that I don't understand at all. It was originally called Mothering Sunday and it was a day that everyone visited their Mother Church. It had nothing whatsoever to do with the person who gave birth to you.

But now, everyone feels under extreme obligation to visit their mother on Mother's Day and not only give them a gift, but also take them out for a meal.

I've even seen men doing this for their wife regardless of whether she has children or not. But the men seem terrified of doing the "wrong thing" and not giving a gift to someone who is not their mother or is not even a mother to anyone.

The whole thing had gotten out of hand. So, every year there's the obligation of gifts and cards for everyone at Christmas, plus a meal together, drinks till late on New Year's Eve, presents and a meal for Valentine's Day, chocolate gifts for Easter and a meal out, gifts and a meal for Mother's Day, and the year's not even half over yet, but you're still stressed and broke. And for what?

I opted out of all this commercial madness years ago, and it was one of the best things I ever did. The bonus is that I get to listen to all the whining and complaining from others who are still caught up in this non-compulsory cycle.

Some of them have joined me in my minimalistic life and opted out of these "traditions." I've always felt that the word tradition is just another word for copying.

As my parents used to tell me when I was a kid and wanted to do what others did, "If they all jumped off a bridge, would you?".

No, I wouldn't, which is why I no longer copy what others do, especially when it detracts from my life in enjoyment, money, and forced activities.

Chapter 13.
A Sufficient Abode

I think that home ownership can be a trap. Don't get me wrong, there's nothing wrong with owning your own home, just owning the wrong home.

Up until the 1990's, it was normal for a family to live in a modest house that was paid for by the father/husband working full-time while the mother/wife looked after the home and family, and maybe had a part time job too.

Sadly, that all changed and now couples want to buy big houses, that are often far too big for the family's needs, and to pay for it, both parents must work full-time which means sticking the kids into childcare at a young age so that someone else can bring them up while they work themselves into exhaustion.

I don't know about you, but I never understood the need for big expensive houses. I think it makes a lot more sense to buy a house that only requires one full-time income to pay for it so that if one parent loses their job, or becomes too incapacitated to work, the other one can work instead.

Not only does this alleviate financial stress, but often, one parent not needing to work full-time means money can be saved by having home-cooked meals, only needing one car, no childcare costs, and more time for each other.

I know that many will disagree with me, but I speak from experience. Two full-time working parents means both are exhausted at the end of the day and have no time to spend with the kids or each other because after work they have to pick up the kids from daycare, make dinner, bathe the kids and get them to bed, have showers themselves, and then it's nearly time for them to go to bed too, so that they can get up and do it all over again the next day, and the next day, and the next day.......

To me that's a living hell and nearly every couple I've ever known who live this way end up getting divorced, because they're so rushed and frustrated and constantly bickering over who does the most at home.

This is why the choice of abode you choose should be sufficient and no more. And by sufficient, I mean it's enough to fit the family comfortably. And contrary to popular opinion, it's not necessary for kids to have their own room. It's okay if they share. A room of their own might be a want, but it's not a need.

I remember when I was a kid, we once lived next door to a family who had seven children (I think it was 7). They weren't exactly children at the time because they were all teenagers and I think one or two of the sons might even have been in their early twenties.

Anyway, they had four daughters and three sons. It may have been two sons, but I'm sure it was three.

What was surprising was that they only had a three-bedroom house. One day they invited our family (of 5) over for dinner, so it was quite a full house of people.

One of the daughters took my sister and I down the hallway to show us her bedroom.

I was stunned. It was a large room, large enough to fit two single beds on each side of the room and four chests of drawers, one next to each bed. The beds had the heads against the wall and the foot of the bed facing the foot of the bed opposite. There was also a built-in wardrobe that had two doors, so all the daughters mustn't have had many hanging clothes. The room was neat and clean, and I guessed that the sons had a similar bedroom with three beds and three chests of drawers. I don't think I've ever seen a bedroom with so many beds in it.

If any of them had an issue with sharing a bedroom like that, they didn't show it. They were an extremely happy and close-knit family. As well as the three bedrooms, their house had one bathroom, one large kitchen/dining room and one living room, plus small verandah's front and back.

As a child I was fascinated that so many people could live in such a small house (small for them) and be so happy and close with each other. It was years later, when I recalled my memory of that family that I wondered if the reason they were such a close family unit was because they lived so physically close to each other, which made for tighter bonds.

When we were there for dinner that night, I noticed how the whole family participated in making the meal, serving it up, and doing the dishes afterwards. And they did it so easily as if each person knew their job because they'd done it so many times before.

They obviously weren't a rich family, but they didn't seem to mind that either. They lived simply and happily together, and their house was so neat and clean, especially considering how many people lived there.

The father worked full-time, and their mother was a busy smiling housewife. She seemed to be on her feet all day taking care of everything. At weekends, when all the family were home together, they too always seemed busy, doing chores in the garden, looking after their cars, or sitting out on the verandah drinking tea and chatting.

Contrast this with families who buy houses far bigger than they need, then have to put their kids in childcare so they can both work full-time and spend their weekends and evenings trying to catch up on all the things that didn't get done through the week, leaving them both exhausted yet having to go back and do it all again the next week.

Don't get me wrong. I'm not suggesting that all women should stay at home while their husbands go out to work. I'm saying that there's no upside to buying a house bigger than you need for more money than you can comfortably afford.

Here's another example of a couple living within their means.

I knew a woman who lived with her husband and young daughter. They were renting cheap accommodation and not spending money, preferring to put it all into savings, so that they could buy a house of their own.

A few years later they had almost enough money to buy a small house. They had really saved hard to do it and had spent nothing for a few years. They didn't even own a car, because her husband could walk to work in good weather or catch a bus if it was raining. She had a part-time local job, so she didn't need a car either. They also lived close to their local shopping centre.

Between them they earned enough to buy food, pay their bills, and save a lot, which they did. They didn't have holidays, didn't eat out, only did free activities (walks, museums, free local exhibitions) and rarely bought clothes. They were extremely disciplined about spending and ate extremely frugally too, which was a healthy diet of rice, beans, and vegetables. They ate plenty of baked potatoes, vegetable lasagna, vegetable casseroles and rice and vegetable salads.

They were impressive in their frugality, but they had a plan and a goal and stuck to it.

I think it was only five or six years later that they almost had enough money to buy a house but needed a tiny mortgage.

They bought a small two-bedroom house with a kitchen/dining room, a living room, one bathroom, and a small yard, front and back.

It wasn't a great house, but it was solid. Over the years that I knew them they made few changes to that house. They paid off their small mortgage within the first year by being as frugal as ever and using what would have been their rent money to help clear the mortgage.

Then they initiated the final part of their plan, which was for them both to only work part-time, and at different times so that there was always one of them free to look after their daughter.

And they did it. Their frugal training over the past few years meant they could live comfortably on two part-time incomes which left them with plenty of time to spend together as a family. They were never financially rich, but they never intended to be. They had enough money for everything they needed, plus they bought a used car, added built-in heating to their house and replaced all the carpets, curtains and flooring. But apart from that their life didn't change, except they went on holiday every year or two, but always out of season and at a heavily discounted price, and they always enjoyed themselves.

So, this couple shows that it's not always a case of one parent working full-time while one stays at home with the kids. Neither of them wanted a 9-5 job, so they found a way that worked for them.

Cheaper costs of living.

Having a smaller house is cheaper in more ways than in the price to buy it.

A home needs heating in winter and colling in summer, and naturally a bigger house will have bigger heating and cooling costs.

As we discussed earlier, you can drastically reduce your electric and gas costs by being aware of how you're using them inefficiently.

With heating and cooling, these are things you need to consider before you buy or rent a property. You also need to consider where the property is. For example, where I live the weather is mostly hot. The climate is sub-tropical so it can get extremely hot and humid in summer, and cold enough to need heaters in winter, because the evenings can get cool.

Also, the cold weather usually only lasts for three months a year, so it's better to have a home that's easy to keep cool. That's why most houses and apartments here have high ceilings and shady verandahs/balconies.

Taking heating and cooling into account can save you hundreds or even thousands of dollars a year. Also, looking at insulated walls/ceilings, rattly windows, ill-fitting doors, and how trees and neighbouring properties will affect how cold or warm your home is, can also make a big difference to your bills.

We used to own a house that had one brick wall that was in full sun all day. In winter it was great for keeping the house warm, but in summer it made the house far too hot. So eventually we planted a bushy tree outside that wall, and it made a huge difference to the inside temperature of the house. Also, it was a lemon tree, so we benefitted from the fruit also. Win-win.

Don't Cater for Guests

I often hear people say that they want to buy a house with a spare bedroom for guests.

Unbelievable.

Buying a room you don't need is crazy.

Just do the math.

The difference in price between a two-bedroom and three-bedroom house can be as much as 50%. The same goes for buying a four-bedroom house, when all you really need is three bedrooms.

If you're considering buying a house with a bedroom you don't need, just in case someone may want to sleep there, just ask yourself (and be honest), how often do you have overnight guests?

That extra bedroom will cost you extra money to decorate it, carpet it, clean it, and furnish it. Plus, to buy it, you'll pay an extra hundred thousand dollars, or more, for the property. And for what? So that someone can come and sleep there a couple of weeks a year?

It would be a lot cheaper to put them up in a hotel or let them have your room and you go sleep on the couch for a couple of weeks or borrow/rent an extra bed and sleep in the garage. You could even rent a caravan and put it in the yard.

Any property that has more rooms than you need is wasteful and in the long run will cost you far more than you'll ever realise.

Go online and use one of those mortgage repayment calculators and you'll see that it only takes an increase in price of fifty thousand dollars, or less, to increase the mortgage payments higher than you could comfortably pay back.

Walk, Don't Ride

They say that the three most important things about buying a property are location, location, location. And it's true.

You'll never be happy living somewhere that means you have a long commute to work. Not only will it make you unhappy, but it costs money. It doesn't matter if you drive to work or take public transport, it's still expensive.

It's better to live within a short commute, or even better, within walking distance. Now I know that living close enough to work is unrealistic for some people, but living closer to work, or on an easier commute (one bus ride instead of one bus, one train, and a short walk) is cheaper and a whole lot easier.

You should also choose somewhere that's in walking distance to conveniences like the local shopping centre.

I'm fortunate that where I live there is a convenience store nearby, plus I'm in walking distance to all the local shops, bars, restaurants, parks, and the beach. I do have a car, but I only use it two or three times a month, to go out of town, to carry heavy purchases, or for a day out.

I know quite a few people who live out in the country, and that's fine for them. They grow some of their food and only shop once a month, so they need to take a list so they don't forget anything. But they still must go to work, and that's where it costs them time and money.

Others who live in the country and don't go out to work, spend most of their time working on their land, which is something that I wouldn't want to do. They also drive into town one evening a week to have dinner or drinks with friends. I guess we're all social creatures at heart.

I prefer a more convenient location so that I can walk everywhere. It's cheaper, healthier for me, and better for the planet.

Chapter 14.
To Work Full-Time or Part-Time

In the last chapter I told you about my friends who wanted to live frugally so that they both could work part-time. And they did it quite successfully.

But what if you live alone, or you're a single parent and you don't have the option of sharing the responsibility of earning an income with a partner? This means that you must go out and work full-time, whether you want to or not.

Well, not necessarily. When it comes to working there are many options of what you can do.

Way back when I was a single parent and could only do minimum-wage jobs, it was then that I decided to change my situation.

At first, I wasn't sure what to do. It was before the internet was really a thing and most people didn't have a computer, so research wasn't easy.

However, I did know that computers were emerging, so I found a free, part-time computer programming course at my local college and started doing that. I wasn't even sure if it was something I really wanted to do, but I figured that as more people started using computers, it wouldn't hurt me to learn more about them. I also found out that the college had a free Word Processing course, so I did that too.

And while I didn't know what I wanted to so, I knew what I didn't want. I didn't want to work for minimum wage, and I didn't want to rent a house.

I wanted to earn double the minimum wage, or more, and I wanted to buy my own home.

Earning more per hour meant having a skill or a degree. I investigated it more and found a training place that would not only teach you a skill, but also find you a job placement.

So, I signed up and worked in their finance office learning to do their accounts. And you know what? It was so boring it taught me that I have no interest in doing accounts. But I still stayed there for the year I'd signed up for while I figured something else out.

It was during that time that I found out about the Open University that let you study for a degree at home, and for unemployed people like me it was free.

I was so happy. I couldn't believe it. I had no idea whatsoever what I wanted to study, but I did know that people with degrees have much more interesting jobs than people doing accounts, and they earn a lot more money.

But before I could begin studying, I needed to get my school grades up to an acceptable level.

I found a local college that did classes for 'mature' students, so I signed up for several classes because I still had no idea where I was going. But I was going.

Two years later I had the grades I needed, and I'd been working part-time doing a bit of cleaning work, so I had some savings too.

I figured that with a degree, I could work full-time and earn a lot, or work part-time and still earn more than a full-time minimum wage job. But at least I was going to be able to choose how much or how little I wanted to work.

As it turned out, while studying for my degree (in history, as it turned out) I also began doing a writing course (from home) because I'd always enjoyed writing and thought that doing some freelance work would be a fun way to earn some extra money.

I was right that it was a good way to earn extra money, but I enjoyed it so much that I wanted to do it for a living. And the rest, as they say, is history (ironically).

So, my story goes to show that you can choose how much you earn and how much you work. For a while I worked full-time and did my freelance writing as a side hustle. Eventually I worked part-time and wrote more until I could quit work altogether and write for a living.

You could do the same. Find something you enjoy doing and do it for a living. I know those who are creative and sell their artwork or other handmade goods online. Some buy and sell things and have an online store.

Others learn a skill they enjoy like programming, app development, web design or coding and do it for a living working from home. They either work for one company or freelance and have several clients.

Once you start looking around at all the different ways you can earn money working for yourself, you'll be amazed as I was at how many different opportunities there are out there. You could become a writer like I did.

I find that writing is not just something I do for a living, it's something I want to do all the time. It's as though it's my calling in life. My mission. I even wrote a book about a 10-step process to finding and living your own life mission, called 'Mission Critical For Life.' There's a link to it at the end of this book.

Working for yourself usually means choosing you own hours to work. This can be really freeing.

At first, it's hard to settle down and work at home because there's no boss cracking a whip, no one to see you getting distracted with social media when you're supposed to be working, and when you're at home it's too easy to think you should be doing other things like cleaning, shopping, and other daily chores. But once you learn the art of self-discipline it gets easy.

I know a guy who's a computer programmer. He spends his days doing whatever he wants or sitting in the garden reading computer programming books. In the evenings, he settles down in front of his computer and works till around midnight.

I also know a writer who likewise spends his days doing whatever he wants and then later in the evening he heads to his study where he writes for hours and finally goes to bed just before most people are getting up, and sleeps till late morning.

Both these guys love the quieter hours for working and having their days free. And there are so many others who work like this too.

I'm more of a morning person, so I like to get up early, get any chores done, and then settle down to my writing for the rest of the day, and into the evening too when I'm working on a big project, or when I'm well and truly in the writing 'flow.'

And if you don't want to work from home, you can study for a degree or learn a high-earning skill.

All these suggestions are ways for you to have more money, not just now, but for the rest of your life.

Choose how much you want to earn, how you're going to earn it, and what it'll take to get started.

They say that if you love what you do, you'll never work a day in your life. And it's true.

But you still need the discipline to do the work that you have to do. Luckily for me I found out what it was that I wanted to do and learned a lot of other things along the way, like computer programming, web design, psychology, and I even took an upholstery and soft-furnishing class. Even now I still read books and have done courses on different types of writing, SEO and marketing, and copywriting. Perhaps I'm just a life-long learner.

But it's not only led me to the job of my dreams, but helped me to keep going and growing.

And you can choose what it is you really want to do too, and then go out and do it.

Or, if you're like I was when I didn't know exactly what I wanted to do, try a few things and you'll quickly discover what you like, what bores you, and what you enjoy doing the most.

You can then work towards your dream job, your desired income, and have a ton of fun doing it.

And when you can earn more an hour than you ever could before, you can then decide how much you want to work.

Having a goal in life and working towards it, is rewarding in so many ways, not just in the goal itself. It gives life much more purpose and satisfaction.

Chapter 15.
Financial Round Up

So now we come to the end of this money-saving adventure, so let's recap a few things plus add one or two more.

The first thing is that if you need money now, selling what you don't need is the fastest way to get it. We all own more than we need, so selling off what we don't need, and what has no sentimental attachment, is not only a fast way to have money, but it frees up your time because the less you own, the less you have to look after.

Budgeting is the next step so that you can control your spending and put more into savings. Some people swear by the 10% saving plan whereby you save 10% of your income and never touch it, and that includes 10% of all your income, even unexpected things like money you win or are given as a gift. And each time your regular income goes up, you increase your 10% accordingly.

Your budget must also include dealing with any debt that you have. And stick to your budget. Even though it may seem hard at first, you'll soon adjust.

No one can help you with your budget because only you know your own circumstances but do what you can in all areas of your life to spend less.

There was a couple I used to follow online called The Frugalwoods. They used to spend as little as possible every week while they saved to buy their dream home. They both worked full time and would always have porridge for breakfast every morning and pack a lunch box of a curried rice and beans for lunch every day.

You can also do something similar to really decrease your day-to-day spending. Even cleaning out the fridge-freezer every week helps you to see what food you need to use up so that nothing gets wasted.

Not giving money away is another great tip. This includes decreasing gift-giving. And never, ever loan money to anyone. If they have money troubles give them some of your best tips, but don't give them any money. They're already in debt so putting them in deeper debt won't help.

Don't buy things you don't need. Always be clear as to whether something is a want or a need. Also look at cost per use. And always take care of what you own so that it lasts longer.

Decrease spending in everything you do. Wash your own car, drive less, put on warmer clothing instead of turning up the heating, open windows in summer and use ceiling fans instead of turning on the air-conditioning.

Go for more free days out. Picnics are much more fun than sitting in a restaurant or café, and far cheaper. If you want to go somewhere expensive, save up.

Buy a smaller home. It's less to heat/cool, less to buy, less to maintain, and means you can pay it off sooner.

Earning more is an easy way to have more money. I was once contemplating joining a gym, but I was unsure as to whether I'd enjoy it or if I'd keep going to it. In the end I had a brilliant idea as to how I could get regular exercise, go every day, and get paid to do it. I got a cleaning job at two of my local banks. I was a genius idea. I got all the exercise I needed, I had to go every night (5 nights/week) and it paid money straight into my savings account every month.

All these are just some of the ways that you can start spending less and saving more.

There's no point going out and earning money year after year if you end up with nothing. You're no better off than someone on welfare.

Spending less and having money saved in the bank gives you financial security.

Save enough money so that you have at least a year's income saved, more if you can. That way, if you lose your job, get injured or too ill to work, you'll have a financial cushion to lean on.

I knew someone who did this and always had more than a year's worth of income saved and was adding to it all the time. He called it a 'screw you' fund and said it gave him peace of mind to know that if his boss ever became difficult with him, he could say "screw you" and leave, knowing he had financial independence for a year or more. It came as no surprise that he eventually saved enough to retire nearly two decades early.

Not only can accruing savings help you to walk away from a job you don't like, or to retire early, it also gives you peace of mind to know that if anything breaks down or needs repairing, you've got the funds to cover it.

And all this financial security comes from spending less on things you don't need.

Have a date night once a month with your spouse, or with yourself if you're single, and review where your money is going and look at ways to improve your financial situation. It's so easy to keep track of it this way.

And remember the ice-cream story that I told you about at the beginning of this book, about my neighbour who was spending two thousand dollars a year buying ice-cream for her two kids every day.

This story demonstrates just how easy it is to waste money. Even the little things can add up to a huge amount.

You don't need a high income to have plenty of money. You just have to live smarter, which includes spending less.

And surprisingly, it's a lot of fun.

End.

Books To Help You Earn Save More

Recalled by Life
By Anthony J Sattilaro
https://amzn.to/3BS2Pgm

The Cancer Survivor's Guide: Foods That Help You Fight Back
By Dr Neal Barnard
https://amzn.to/3A3Jlnr

The $21 Challenge: Save $300 in a week! No coupons required!
By Fiona Lippey
https://amzn.to/3BRqptj

The Millionaire Next Door: The Surprising Secrets of America's Wealthy
By Thomas J Stanley
https://amzn.to/3BM6Hzk

Mission Critical For Life: Start Living Life On Your Terms By Pursuing Your True Life Mission
By Ruth Barringham
https://ruthiswriting.com/books/MCFL.html

www.ingramcontent.com/pod-product-compliance
Lightning Source LLC
Chambersburg PA
CBHW050320010526
44107CB00055B/2321